Law Made Fun through Downton Abbey

LESSONS IN LAW FROM THE CAPTIVATING TV SERIES

This book is not authorized, prepared, approved, licensed or endorsed by the Public Broadcasting Service, Julian Fellowes, or any other individual or entity associated with the Downton Abbey TV show.

The second book in the Law Made Fun series.

KAREN MORRIS, ESQ.
SANDRA WILLIAMS, ESQ.

Law Made Fun through Downton Abbey

Lessons in Law from the Captivating TV Series

Karen Morris Esq. & Sandra Williams Esq.

Copyright 2016 by Karen Morris Esq. & Sandra Williams Esq. All rights reserved. Printed in the United States of America. No Part of this book may be used or reproduced in any matter whatsoever without written permission except in the case of brief quotations embodied in critical articles or reviews.
ISBN: 1537574558
ISBN 13: 9781537574554

For information contact judgekaren@aol.com.
For more information, see www.lawmadefun.com
and www.judgekaren.com.

Cover design by Christina Nasello, NVus Designs
First Edition: August, 2016
To be printed by CreateSpace

Dedication

I dedicate this book to Helene Orenstein, a fellow Downton Abbey devotee and a long-time friend who lives in my favorite city, Las Vegas. Helene was the person who introduced me to the riveting TV show, Downton Abbey. Together we lament its denouement.

Karen Morris

About The Authors

Karen Morris is a lawyer, a textbook author, a Distinguished Professor of Law in Rochester, New York, and an elected Town Judge. She is jazzed by the Downton Abbey series and by sharing her passion for law.

Sandra Williams is an attorney and an adjunct Professor of Law.

Table of Contents

About The Authors · vii
Introduction · xiii
        How to use this book · xiv
        Appendices · xiv

WILLS AND ESTATES · 1
Chapter 1   Entail and Primogeniture – The Earl of Grantham and Mathew · · 3
Chapter 2   Contingent Beneficiary – Mathew · 6
Chapter 3   Wills: Renouncing a Bequest – Mathew · · · · · · · · · · · · · · · · · · · 8
Chapter 4   Trusts – Martha Levinson · 10
Chapter 5   Child Out of Wedlock – Ethel and Edith · · · · · · · · · · · · · · · · · · 12

FAMILY RELATIONSHIPS · 15
Chapter 6   Adoption and Guardianship – Edith, Marigold, and Mrs. Drew · · 17
Chapter 7   Interracial Marriage – Lady Rose and Jack Ross · · · · · · · · · · · · · 20
Chapter 8   War Brides – Daisy · 22
Chapter 9   Birth Control – Mary · 24
Chapter 10 Separation – Susan and Shrimpy Macclare · · · · · · · · · · · · · · · · 26
Chapter 11 Divorce: Impotency as Grounds – Mathew · · · · · · · · · · · · · · · · 28

Chapter 12 Divorce: Insanity as Grounds – Michael Gregson · · · · · · · · · · · · · ·30
Chapter 13 Annulment: Fraud – Edna Braithwaite · 32
Chapter 14 Relinquishment of Parental Rights – Ethel Parks · · · · · · · · · · · · · · 33
Chapter 15 Rights of a Fetus – O'brien and Cora ·36
Chapter 16 Medical Privacy – Lady Sybil and Dr. Ryder · · · · · · · · · · · · · · · · · · · 38
Chapter 17 Nuremberg Laws – Rose and Atticus ·40

BUSINESS LAW · 43
Chapter 18 Americans with Disabilities Act – Mr. Bates · · · · · · · · · · · · · · · · · · 45
Chapter 19 Bankruptcy – Robert ·47
Chapter 20 Contracts: Condition Precedent – Joseph Molesley · · · · · · · · · · · · 50
Chapter 21 Contracts: Exculpatory Clauses – Titanic Passengers · · · · · · · · · · · ·51
Chapter 22 Contract Law: Restaurant Reservations – Anna and Mr. Bates · · · 53
Chapter 23 Contracts: Revocation of an Offer – Mr. Carson and
            Joseph Molesley · 55
Chapter 24 Employment: Interview Questions – Phyllis Baxter · · · · · · · · · · · · 57
Chapter 25 Employment: Letters of Recommendation – Edna Braithwaite · · · 59
Chapter 26 Negligence: Respondeat Superior – Titanic · · · · · · · · · · · · · · · · · · · 61
Chapter 27 Partnerships – Mathew and Robert ·64
Chapter 28 Warranties – Mr. Bates · 66

CRIMINAL LAW – SPECIFIC CRIMES ·69
Chapter 29 Elements of a Crime – Investigator Vyner · 71
Chapter 30 Arson – Branson ·73
Chapter 31 Bribery – Harold Levinson · 74
Chapter 32 Trespass and Burglary – Terence Sampson · 76
Chapter 33 Conspiracy – Durant and Craig · 78
Chapter 34 Endangering the Welfare of a Child – Nanny West · · · · · · · · · · · · ·80
Chapter 35 Extortion and Coercion – Vera Bates · 82
Chapter 36 Forgery – Mr. Bates ·84

Chapter 37	Impersonation – Major Patrick Gordon	86
Chapter 38	Larceny – Thomas	88
Chapter 39	Murder and Manslaughter – Titanic Crew	89
Chapter 40	Promoting Prison Contraband – Durant and Craig	91
Chapter 41	Social Gambling – Terence Sampson and Michael Gregson	92
Chapter 42	Sodomy and Related Sex Crimes – Thomas	94
Chapter 43	Speeding – Mathew	96
Chapter 44	Spitting – Train Station	98
Chapter 45	Tampering with a Witness – Audrey Bartlett	100
Chapter 46	Tampering with Evidence – Mary	102
Chapter 47	Terrorism – Branson	104

CRIMINAL LAW PROCEDURE · · · · · · 107

Chapter 48	Alibi – Mr. Bates	109
Chapter 49	Circumstantial Evidence – John Pegg and Vera Bates	111
Chapter 50	Exoneration: Post Conviction Relief – Mr. Bates	113
Chapter 51	Death Penalty – Mr. Bates	115
Chapter 52	False Confessions – Mr. Bates	117
Chapter 53	Handwriting Experts – Terence Sampson	118
Chapter 54	Police Line-Ups – Anna	120
Chapter 55	Prison Mail – Mr. Bates	122

MISCELLANEOUS · · · · · · 125

Chapter 56	Conscientious Objector – Branson	127
Chapter 57	Conversion Therapy – Thomas	129
Chapter 58	Deed of Transference – Cora	131
Chapter 59	Eviction – Timothy Drewe	133
Chapter 60	Free Speech: Fighting Words – Branson	135
Chapter 61	Medical Malpractice: Failure to Diagnose – Dr. Tapsell	137
Chapter 62	Voting Rights for Women – Edith	139

APPENDICES 141
Appendix A Introduction to Law 143
Appendix B Wills and Estates 145
Appendix C Differences Between Civil and Criminal Law 147
Appendix D Criminal Law Issues 149
Appendix E Court Jurisdiction 151

Introduction

Welcome fellow Downton Abbey fans! If you love the intrigue, drama and humor of life's relationships portrayed in the popular TV series, and if you are curious about the law, this book is for you. It explores the intersection of Downton Abbey's characters and the law of our society. You may have seen all the episodes, perhaps more than once, and not realized that the story lines touch upon many legal principles. Or you may have identified legal matters in the show but never knew if they were true-to-life. This book will expand your encounter with the Crawleys and everyone in their world, and also your horizons, by teaching you the law using the world of Downton Abbey as your guide.

For a society to function orderly and for people to live together without chaos, there must be laws and rules for people to follow. Thus, law is a critical component for any civilized society, including ours and that of Downton Abbey. This book uses the twists and turns in the experiences of our favorite, and some not-so-favorite, characters as case examples to illustrate legal principles.

How to use this book

This book contains seven sections, six of which cover a major category of law and consist of numerous chapters that each address that area of law. The chapters include the following components.

* **CHAPTER TITLES**

    The titles identify the issue of law discussed in each chapter, and also the main Downton Abbey character portrayed in the relevant vignette.

* **DA FACTS**

    This section contains Downton Abbey story sketches relevant to the particular law addressed in the chapter. "DA" refers to Downton Abbey.

* **US LAW**

    This feature provides easily understood explanations of the law of the United States.

* **APPLICATION TO DA**

    This part discusses the US law's application to the show's characters and storylines. This information eases the learning process by involving plots and characters that fascinate us all.

Appendices

The seventh section occurs at the end of the book and consists of five **APPENDICES** that provide detailed information regarding some of the terms and laws discussed throughout the chapters. If you are new to the study of law, you are well-advised to read the **APPENDICES** first. They provide a good framework on which to absorb the rest of the book.

One of the exciting, yet confounding, characteristics of the law is that it frequently changes. Legislators pass new statutes, and judges interpret the rules with new insights. The law discussed in this book relates to the law in effect as of the time of publication.

Whenever a legal term is used, it is printed in italics and a definition follows. This book is a legalese-free zone.

For ease of reading, we have used the pronoun "he" throughout the book in lieu of the somewhat awkward alternatives of "he or she" or "s/he". Ideally, a pronoun referring to one person would exist that is gender-neutral, but such is not the case. So please know that our use of "he" is intended, like the law, to be all inclusive.

So come extend your encounter with the popular television series and add an additional dimension to your fondness for the Crawleys and their servants – lessons in law from the life and times of the residents of Downton Abbey. Enjoy!

Genealogy of Robert Crawley
Earl of Grantham

- **Robert's Great Grandfather** — Prior Earl of Grantham
  - **Robert's Grandfather** — Prior Earl of Grantham
    - **Robert's Uncle** — Robert's Father's Younger Brother
      - **James Crawley** — Robert's Cousin
        - **Patrick Crawley**
    - **Robert's Father** — Prior Earl of Grantham
      - **Robert Crawley** — Earl of Grantham & **Cora** — Countess of Grantham
        - **Matthew Crawley** — Robert's Third Cousin, Removed & **Mary**
          - **George Crawley**
        - **Edith**
        - **Sybil** & **Branson**
          - **Sybbie Branson** (Female)

Wills and Estates

Chapter 1

Entail and Primogeniture – The Earl of Grantham and Mathew

DA FACTS: The estate encompassing Downton Abbey was subject to an entail. The owner of the entail was the Earl of Grantham.

BRITISH LAW *(Note: This chapter refers to British law. It is one of only two chapters in which law from a country other than the United States is discussed. The reason here is the central role the English law of entail plays throughout the Downton Abbey series.[1])*: *Entail* means property cannot be subdivided, cannot be split among heirs, and cannot be taken by creditors to satisfy debts. Rather, the estate remains intact and passes to a beneficiary determined by the rules of entail. This is generally a first born male in the main line of family succession.

The rights of an owner of entailed property are quite different than owners of property not subject to entail. The effect of the entail is that the owner can enjoy the property for his lifetime but subsequent owners are predetermined. A current owner has no right to determine future owners. A current owner cannot sell the property or *devise* it (give it away in a will). In effect, a current owner

---

[1] The other chapter is 17 concerning Roe's marriage to Atticus who is Jewish. The chapter addresses the Nuremberg Laws of Germany adopted in 1935.

of entailed property holds it in trust for future generations, and has a legal duty to preserve the property for them.

An adjunct to entail in England through the early 20th century was primogeniture, the rule of law that holds that only sons, and not daughters, can inherit. Since the property could not be split or shared, the oldest son inherited all the property. A lucky fluke of birth for the eldest son. And even if he had an older sister, she was bypassed and he received all.

Titles, such as King and Earl, could also be entailed.

An example of a title subject to entail and primogeniture is provided by none other than the creator of Downton Abbey, Julian Fellowes. His wife is the niece of an English earl whose title was entailed. The uncle died childless in 2011. But for primogeniture, Mrs. Fellowes would have inherited the title. Since she is female, she is not eligible. Perhaps this circumstance inspired the whole series.

The English crown was subject to entail and primogeniture. A princess could inherit the throne if and only if she has no brothers. Thus, the current Queen of England reigns. If she had a male sibling, even a younger one, he would have trumped her. Time marches on and circumstances change. For decades the country had been talking about a change to its constitution to treat royal sons and daughters equally in succession to the throne, yet no action was taken. Speculation attributes this to the fact that, for the next two generations, a change would be moot, given Price Charles, Prince William and Prince Henry waiting in the wings.

Once Prince William and Duchess Kate Middleton announced their intention to start a family, strong impetus existed to address the gender succession issue with legislation. In 2013, Parliament passed the Succession to the Crown Act which altered the laws of succession to the British throne by eliminating the male-preference. The effect would be that a first-born girl would have precedence over a younger brother. Since we now know that the Duke and Duchess' first born is a boy, the new law may have to wait at least another generation for a practical application.

ADDITIONAL DA FACTS: Robert and Cora Crawley had three lovely daughters – Mary, Edith and Sybil, and no sons.

ENGLISH LAW: If the current owner of property that is subject to entail has no sons, as was the case with Robert Crawley, the property reverts to the closest eldest living male. True, even if that person is a distant relative.

APPLICATION TO DA: Please see the genealogy chart three pages back. Because Robert and Cora had no sons, upon Robert's death Downton Abbey reverts to the closest eldest living male who takes ownership through his father, and not his mother. The qualifying male was James Crawley, Robert's cousin. James was the oldest living son of Robert's father's younger brother (Robert's uncle). When James died, his only son Patrick would have inherited. But alas, fate took its course and the two died aboard the Titanic. The next closest qualifying family member was Robert's third cousin once removed who we came to know as Mathew.

As we know, Mathew was quite surprised when he received notice that he was in line to inherit. He did not know the family, the estate, or the area. But he was the presumptive inheritor of the Downton Abbey mansion. Such is entail and primogeniture.

Chapter 2

Contingent Beneficiary – Mathew

FACTS: Mathew received a letter from a lawyer advising him that he was named the second contingent heir to the substantial estate of Lavinia's father, Reginald Swire. Despite Mathew's remote position, he did inherit the money. Turns out the primary beneficiary predeceased Reginald, and the second was missing in India.

US LAW: When writing a will, the *testator* (person writing the will) can designate *primary beneficiaries* and *contingent beneficiaries*. A *beneficiary* is a person, business or organization designated by the testator to receive money or property after death. A primary beneficiary is first in line to receive the assets. A contingent beneficiary is typically someone who is designated to receive an inheritance only if the primary beneficiary dies before the testator or cannot be found.

An heir who cannot be located is called a *missing heir*. The person responsible for settling the estate, called an *executor*, must make a genuine effort to find the missing heir. While the hunt is underway, the money must be held in trust by the executor and not distributed for a period of time determined by state law. For example, some states require the bequest be held for three years. If the missing heir is not found by the expiration of the designated time, the contingent beneficiary is entitled to the money.

A testator can list in the will numerous contingent beneficiaries but to avoid confusion, the intended order should be clearly stated.

APPLICATION TO DA: Mathew was a second contingent beneficiary. Lucky for him, the primary beneficiary died before Reginald. The *bequest* (a gift of money or property in a will) would thus be paid to the first contingent beneficiary. However, Mathew's luck continued. The first contingent beneficiary was last known to have travelled to India and could not be located despite a good faith effort by the executor. Therefore, Mathew inherited the money.

Chapter 3

Wills: Renouncing a Bequest – Mathew

A FACTS: Following Lavinia's death, her father Reginald Swire, was left with no immediate family. His wife, Lavinia's mother, had predeceased him long before. Lavinia was their only child. The father, a London solicitor (lawyer), died soon after Lavinia. He left his estate to Mathew, who was Lavinia's fiancée at the time of her death. Mathew initially wanted to decline the inheritance because he felt guilty about Lavinia's death, believing he contributed to it by breaking her heart and her will to live when she became ill with the Spanish flu.

About that time, Lord Grantham learned that an investment he made in a Canadian railroad company, using most of Downton Abbey's funds, went sour, leaving Downton Abbey potentially destitute. Mary, then Mathew's fiancée and soon his wife, believed the inheritance could save Downton Abbey. The two argued, Mary insisting he accept it and Mathew wanting to decline the inheritance or give the money to charity. However, a letter was discovered written by Lavinia to Reginald advising him prior to his making the bequest to Mathew of the status of Lavinia and Mathew's relationship. Guilt assuaged, Mathew accepted the money and applied it to running Downton Abbey. In exchange, he became a co-owner with Robert.

US LAW: A beneficiary in a will can *renounce* the *bequest* (gift in a will), meaning voluntarily decline or refuse to accept the gift. One reason this might be done is to avoid tax liabilities associated with the gift. Another reason would apply where the beneficiary is in debt. If he inherited, the money would go to the creditors. By disclaiming the debtor's interest, the money will go to other beneficiaries instead. When a renunciation occurs, the bequest usually reverts back to the estate and is distributed to other beneficiaries as though the renouncing beneficiary had died before the *testator*, meaning the person who wrote the will. Typically, a renunciation must be made in writing, describe the property being renounced, and be filed with the appropriate court within a time frame specified by state statute.

APPLICATION TO DA: Had Mathew decided to renounce his bequest from Reginald, he could have done so. Fortunately for the inhabitants of Downton Abbey, Mathew changed his mind and accepted the much-needed money.

Chapter 4

Trusts – Martha Levinson

FACTS: The Crawley family realized that Downton Abbey was in dire financial straits. Lady Mary decided to invite her maternal grandmother, Martha Levinson, a resident of the United States, to visit Downton. Mary hoped that she would invest in it, as Cora had done years before when she married Robert.

When Mary eventually asked her grandmother for the money to save Downton Abbey, Mrs. Levinson advised that, although her deceased husband had left her a generous allowance, the capital generating the funds was in a *trust* and she had no authority to control the principal. That fact notwithstanding, Mrs. Levinson questioned the wisdom of saving Downton, believing such large estates were meant for an earlier era. Instead, she invited the Crawleys to occupy her houses in New York and Newport.

US LAW: A trust is an arrangement in which money is managed by a person called a trustee for the benefit of another, called a *beneficiary*. Trusts are often created in a person's will for one of two primary reasons. The first is that trusts can help to reduce the amount of estate taxes following a person's death. A trust also provides a means to limit access to large sums of money by a beneficiary who is known to be a spendthrift or is otherwise incapable of wise spending due perhaps to age or mental incapacity.

The person creating the trust typically provides directions to the trustee concerning the circumstances under which money from the trust can be transferred to the beneficiary. Examples include: to provide an allowance at regular intervals for living expenses; to cover medical needs; to pay school tuition; etc. If the reason for the trust is youth and immaturity of the beneficiary, the trust might specify an age at which the beneficiary is entitled to receive the principal outright, thereby ending the trust.

APPLICATION TO DA: Cora's father left his money in trust for the benefit of his wife, Cora's mother. As a result, Martha did not have control of the inheritance and so could not use it to contribute to Downton Abbey. We can only guess what her husband's motivation was for not giving her the money outright. Is it possible he concurred with his wife about large English estates being out-of-date and, anticipating Downton Abbey's dire circumstances, sought to protect his money? In any event, he successfully prevented its use to save the mansion.

Chapter 5

Child Out of Wedlock – Ethel and Edith

A FACTS: Ethel, a maid, had a sexual liaison with an officer, Major Bryant. After he learned she became pregnant from the encounter, he rejected her. Thereafter, he was killed near the end of the war. Ethel attempted to raise the child on her own, but poverty and the challenges of parenting thwarted her efforts.

Lady Edith also gave birth to a child *out of wedlock* (born to unmarried parents). She had a romantic relationship with the married Michael Gregson, resulting in the birth of much-loved Marigold.

US LAW: In earlier times, a woman who bore a child without the benefit of marriage was scorned and often relegated to a life of shame. Her child was labeled illegitimate and treated by the law as an outcast. The primary legal disabilities of such a child included ineligibility to inherit from the father, and disqualification for child support from the father. Today, those laws are a thing of the past. In a series of cases decided by the United States Supreme Court, the inferior legal status was held to violate the Equal Protection Clause of the United States Constitution. All states now have statutes that protect children born out of wedlock. They are entitled to inherit from their parents on equal grounds as children born during a marriage. They also have the right to require a suspected father to submit to a blood test and, if paternity is confirmed, to financial support.

APPLICATION TO DA: Ethel's unfortunate financial position would be somewhat ameliorated by the law's requirement that unwed fathers contribute to the financial expenses of their children. When Major Bryant died in service, the child would be eligible to inherit from his estate. The added income might have enabled Ethel to afford to keep the child, avoiding the traumatic transfer of de facto custody to the child's grandparents.

Family Relationships

Chapter 6

Adoption and Guardianship – Edith, Marigold, and Mrs. Drew

DA FACTS[2]: Edith became pregnant from an affair with Michael Gregson, and gave birth out of wedlock. This circumstance was scandalous for a single woman living in the times of Downton Abbey. Edith first considered aborting the child but was convinced by her Aunt Rosamund to hide the pregnancy and place the child for adoption. Edith was able to hide the pregnancy with the help of family members, and various schemes. One of those plans was to permit an adoption of the child by a Swiss couple. This Edith did but regretted the decision almost immediately and retrieved the child, no doubt to the great disappointment of the adoptive parents.

Edith preferred to place her child with a local family with the hope of seeing the child with some regularity. She befriended Mr. Drew, a pig farmer at Downton Abbey. He was aware of the true facts; Mrs. Drew was not. The wife was told the child's parents were dead. She assumed Marigold would be permanently a part of her family and bonded accordingly. Edith sought to continue playing a part in Marigold's life as a "friend." When Edith decided to take the child back, Mrs. Drew was understandably devastated and angry.

---

2 This situation is also examined from a different legal perspective in Chapter Five.

Karen Morris Esq. & Sandra Williams Esq.

US LAW: *Adoption* is a legal proceeding before a judge that results in an adopted child having new parent(s). The birth parents' legal status as parents is fully and permanently terminated. Those rights and responsibilities are transferred in full to the adoptive parents. An adopted child acquires the rights of a natural child, and the adoptive parents acquire the rights and duties of biological parents, primarily the right of custody and the obligation of support.

Adoption and revocation of adoption are controlled by state law. Those laws vary considerably from state to state. In New York, for example, adoption is irrevocable 30-45 days after the biological parent(s) signs and transfers the child to the adoptive parents. In other states the time period varies from a few days to even a few years, but only if the consent for the adoption given by the biological parents was obtained by fraud.

The time before the adoption becomes irrevocable is called the *revocable period*. If a biological parent attempts to revoke during the revocable period and the adoptive parent(s) chooses to contest the revocation, the child is not necessarily returned to the birth parent. Instead, a "best interests" hearing is held and the judge determines which would-be parent is consistent with the child's best chance to thrive.

In assessing best interests, judges analyze such factors as the ability, capacity, fitness and readiness of the parties to take parental responsibility, whether the parent(s) have a stable relationship and present a healthy family life, and whether they can provide a loving and secure environment in which the child can feel safe and cared for. Another factor considered is the length of time the child has been living with the adopting family. The longer that period, the more comfortable and settled the child is likely to be there. Another important consideration is the relationship between the child and the adoptive parents.

A legal status short of adoption is guardianship. This is the situation where the court gives authority to an adult to take responsibility temporarily for the care of a child. A court might appoint a guardian where a child's parents are ill and unable to care for him, or his parents are deceased, or the child is awaiting adoptive parents. In such circumstances the court's order appointing the guardian specifies the guardian's duties and responsibilities. Typically a guardian is a family member or family friend, if available.

Today the stigma attached to unwed mothers has dissipated so Edith might have chosen to openly give birth and parent Marigold, thereby avoiding much of the tortuous path she pursued.

APPLICATION TO DA: For Edith to cancel the original adoption, a court would have to hold a hearing to determine whether the child's welfare would be best served by terminating the adoption or leaving the child with the adoptive family. Concerning the Drews, the arrangement was informal without an in-court proceeding. Therefore, whether Mrs. Drew acquired any legal rights to Marigold is doubtful and so Edith, as the biological parent, would likely be entitled legally to retrieve the child.

Chapter 7

Interracial Marriage – Lady Rose and Jack Ross

DA FACTS: Lady Rose MacClare dated the attractive, dapper, and talented jazz musician Jack Ross. She informed Lady Mary that she intended to marry him. Lady Mary, concerned about public condemnation of Rose for marrying across racial lines, spoke with the pianist about her concerns. He concurred that the union would have many detractors and lamented if only this were a "better world."

US LAW: At the time of Downton Abbey, every state but two made it a crime to marry a person of another race. Such marriages were void, meaning in the eyes of the law they never occurred. These laws were generally classified as miscegenation laws. Virginia, not atypically, called its statute, "An Act to Preserve Racial Integrity." The two exceptions were Michigan, which had such a law but repealed it in 1883, and Ohio, which repealed its statute in 1887.

In the 1940's through the 1960's, many states repealed their miscegenation rules. In 1967, sixteen states still had such a law. In that year the United States Supreme Court decided the case of *Loving v. Virginia* which formally invalidated such laws. The case arose from the marriage of a black woman and a white man, Richard Loving. They were married where such unions were legal but then moved to Virginia which still retained its Act to Preserve Racial integrity. The couple was prosecuted and convicted of violating the statute. They were sentenced to a year in jail, but the judge agreed to suspend the sentence if they left Virginia and remained away for at least 25 years(!).

The Supreme Court not only overturned their conviction and state banishment, but included in the decision the following, "The freedom to marry, or not marry, a person of another race resides with the individual, and cannot be infringed by the State."

The effect of the decision was to overturn all remaining state laws that prohibited interracial marriage.

APPLICATION TO DA: If Lady Rose had married Jack Ross, the effect of the ceremony would depend on the state where the marriage occurred. Had she said "I do" in any state but Michigan or Ohio, the marriage would have been void and both parties would be considered single, never married. If Rose married the pianist today, the marriage would, appropriately, be valid in all 50 states.

Chapter 8

War Brides – Daisy

A FACTS: William, the second footman, had a strong attraction to Daisy, an assistant cook, which she did not reciprocate. He proposed to her before leaving to fight in World War I. Daisy rebuffed his romantic overtures. At the warfront he was seriously injured. Doctors declared that he would not survive. William again asked Daisy to marry him before he died so he could experience marriage before his life ended, and so she could receive his pension. Daisy is convinced by Mrs. Patmore and William's father to say "I do." William died six or seven hours following the exchange of nuptials.

US LAW: During wartime, marriage to soldiers was viewed by some women as a way to obtain allotment checks (a designated portion of a military employee's salary paid automatically to a spouse and matched by the government) and a pension. Indeed, some woman engaged in *bigamy* (marrying more than one spouse) to maximize their take. These so-called brides were labeled Fake War Brides, Allotment Annies, and War-Marriage Vampires. The most deceitful of these wives was found to have 12 (12!) husbands.

Mail carriers were enlisted in the effort to identify and stop the offending women. The checks were mailed by the Treasury Department. Multiple envelopes to the same address could raise suspicion prompting the mail carrier to notify the authorities.

Typically, the wrongdoers were the women but in some circumstances the soldiers were participants in the scheme. They claimed nonexistent wives and children to secure government checks.

Another misuse of marriage was for the purpose of circumventing immigration restrictions. As an accommodation to the men in uniform, the government sought to facilitate the entry into the United States of soldiers' brides who hailed from other countries. The War Brides Act, adopted after World War II, gave alien spouses, natural children, and adopted children of US military personnel preferences to enter the US. More than 100,000 entered this way. The Alien Fiancées and Fiancés Act of 1946 extended the privileges to the betrothed of war veterans.

A 1953 case before the United States Supreme Court, *Lutwak v. US*, upheld convictions of *conspiracy* (two or more people acting together to commit a crime) to violate the War Brides Act. The defendants arranged for the fraudulent marriages of three Polish refugees for the purpose of securing their immigration to this country. A key fact that led to prosecution was that the couples never lived together.

APPLICATION TO DA: The circumstances look suspicious because the wedding occurred literally on William's deathbed. Tying the knot so close to a soldier's death suggests the bride's motivation is something other than love and desire to spend her life with the man. However, Daisy's motivation for marrying William was not to receive his pension but rather to grant a dying wish. Thus, Daisy did not qualify as a gold digger violating the law.

Chapter 9

Birth Control – Mary

A FACTS: Lady Mary sent her maid, Anna, to the apothecary to purchase a birth control device. At the time, condoms were the most commonly used method of birth control for men, while women used pessaries. These were rudimentary diaphragms.

Lady Mary read about various birth control measures in a book she kept in her night stand drawer. The author, Marie Stopes, was a scientist who, in real life, became Britain's most accomplished sex educator and contraception advocate.

US LAW: In 1873 Congress passed the Act for the Suppression of Trade in and Circulation of Obscene Literature and Articles of Immoral Use, also called the Comstock Law. This federal statute made it illegal to use the United States Postal Service to send mail that contained information about birth control.

Changes were slow until Planned Parenthood was formed after World War I. From 1914-1945 birth control advocates sought to change the Comstock Law. In 1936 a break-through case occurred. In *United States v. One Package of Japanese Pessaries*, the country sought a court order directing the forfeiture, confiscation and destruction of a package containing rubber pessaries for the prevention of conception imported into the US. A federal Court of Appeals held that physicians may prescribe contraceptives to married women to cure or prevent disease. The court therefore ruled that the Comstock statute should be interpreted reasonably to permit importation of contraception devices where they have a legitimate use.

The biggest change came in 1965 with the high court's decision in *Griswold v. Connecticut*. That decision invalidated a state statute that prohibited any person from using any "drug, medicinal article or instrument for the purpose of preventing conception." Today, contraception devices are of course legal. Some are available over the counter and some require a prescription.

APPLICATION TO DA: Under the Comstock Law, Anna could have been arrested for her purchase of a birth control device. Today, Anna and Lady Mary are legally entitled to buy or be prescribed many different kinds of contraceptive devices.

Chapter 10

Separation – Susan and Shrimpy Macclare

A FACTS: Lady Rose MacClare was the youngest child of Hugh (nicknamed Shrimpy) and Susan MacClare. Susan was Robert's first cousin, making Lady Rose the great niece of Violet Crawley. Susan and Hugh were mismatched and neither was happy in the marriage. They constantly bickered. A major topic of disagreement was parenting the young, blossoming and challenging Lady Rose. Hugh confided in Robert about how troublesome his marriage was. When Hugh was named Governor of Bombay, the couple moved to India. A change in venue did not affect a change in their deteriorating marriage and so they made a mutual decision to separate once they returned to England.

US LAW: *Separation* occurs when a husband and a wife decide to live separate and apart from each other. The parties can agree to separate for any reason or no reason. A separation does not end the marriage; only a divorce does that. Therefore, parties who are separated cannot remarry.

Each state regulates the grounds and conditions for a *legal separation*, meaning a separation granted by order of a court. If one spouse wants a separation, and the other does not, the disillusioned spouse can sue for separation and must prove grounds. They vary from state to state, and typically include cruel and inhuman treatment (physical attacks, forced sex, verbal abuse or intimidation, physical abuse of the couple's child), adultery, gross refusal or neglect to provide suitable support and maintenance, and incarceration for three years or more.

A court order of separation will likely address some of the same issues as a divorce, such as child custody, child visitation, property division (allocation of assets), division of debts, and separation maintenance (spousal and child support).

Some couples discover they are happier without their spouse and so the separation leads to a divorce. Others discover life is better with their other half and so they cancel the separation and reinstitute cohabitation.

APPLICATION TO DA: Lord and Lady MacClare will be seeking a separation. Likely they are both in agreement that the match is not made in heaven and can agree to separate, so that no grounds are needed. If they cannot agree to part ways, the only grounds that might apply is cruel and inhuman treatment via verbal abuse and intimidation. Certainly Susan verbally snipes at Hugh with regularity. Whether her sharp tongue rises to the level of cruel and inhuman treatment would be a question for a judge if she refused to agree to a separation and if Hugh proceeded in court on cruel and inhuman grounds.

Chapter 11

Divorce: Impotency as Grounds – Mathew

A FACTS: Mathew Crawley was engaged to marry Lavinia Swire. Mathew, a valiant fighter in World War I, came home from the battlefield seriously injured. He was diagnosed with spinal damage causing possible permanent paraplegia preventing him from ever walking again. He was told his paralysis caused impotence. Lavinia is undeterred. She loved him and was willing to marry him despite the injuries.

US LAW: Impotency is defined as a physical or psychological condition that prevents one spouse from physically having intercourse with the other. For a male, it includes, but is not limited to, the inability to have and maintain an erection. Inhibiting physical conditions in a woman would also qualify. For both males and females, a psychological condition that blocks the opportunity for intimacy with one's spouse likewise qualifies.

More than half the states include impotency as a ground for divorce or annulment of a marriage. Some states require that a spouse be impotent at the time the couple marries, while others permit a divorce if impotency occurs during the marriage. In some states, a divorce or annulment will be granted only if the impotence is permanent and incurable.

A spouse seeking a divorce or annulment on impotency grounds must prove the condition by medical evidence, either relevant documents and/or the testimony of a qualified medical professional.

Note: Intentionally withholding sexual relations from a spouse, as well as infertility, do not constitute impotence.

APPLICATION TO DA: Lavinia is entitled to marry whoever she wishes and this is so regardless of the condition of her spouse. If she had married Michael and later changed her mind about the type of marriage she wanted or her interest in having children, her entitlement to a divorce or annulment would depend on the law of the state in which she lives.

Chapter 12

Divorce: Insanity as Grounds – Michael Gregson

A FACTS: Michael Gregson, editor of the Sketch in London, was enamored with Lady Edith Crawley but he was married. His wife, who he had adored, developed a mental illness and resided in a mental hospital. She no longer even recognized Gregson. He desired to pursue a relationship with Edith and so wanted a divorce. However, English law barred divorce from a *lunatic* wife, meaning in law insane. He therefore left for Germany where the divorce laws were more lenient.

US LAW: *Divorce* is the legal termination of a marriage. The circumstances that will cause a court to grant a dissolution vary from state to state. At a trial for divorce, the person seeking it must state a legally valid reason for the divorce and be able to establish through testimony and evidence that the reason is well-founded. Many states include as one of the grounds incurable insanity. Necessary proof includes testimony from a medical or psychiatric expert. Some states require a minimum time period during which the condition has lasted. In several states, that time is five years or more.

In some states, insanity is grounds for an *annulment* rather than a divorce if the mental condition existed at the time the marriage began. An annulment ends a marriage by declaring it was invalid from the beginning. In effect, a valid marriage never occurred.

APPLICATION TO DA: Gregson's wife was in an institution due to her mental incompetency. It progressed so far that she did not recognize him. Given these circumstances, Gregson should have no trouble providing the necessary evidence to establish her insanity, and would be entitled to a divorce or annulment, depending on the facts and the state.

Chapter 13

Annulment: Fraud – Edna Braithwaite

FACTS: Lady Cora's new lady's maid Edna Braithwaite forced herself sexually upon Branson when he was intoxicated. She falsely claimed to be pregnant as a result, and urged Branson to marry her. Her ploy was discovered by Mrs. Hughes, and Edna was fired.

US LAW: A false claim of pregnancy for the purpose of convincing the father to marry the pregnant woman constitutes *fraud*. A resulting marriage is voidable, meaning the victim of the misrepresentation can annul the marriage. *Annulment* refers to a court order declaring a marriage void, as though it never occurred. To prove fraud, plaintiff must prove that defendant made an untruthful statement that was a material (significant) fact, plaintiff relied on the alleged fact, plaintiff would not have engaged in certain conduct except for having relied on the misrepresentation, and plaintiff suffered a loss.

APPLICATION TO DA: Had Branson married Edna, the reason would have been that he was misled to believe she was carrying a child he fathered. This constitutes fraud by Edna and would have enabled Branson to annul the marriage once he learned the truth.

Chapter 14

Relinquishment of Parental Rights – Ethel Parks

DA FACTS: Ethel Parks was a housemaid at Downton Abbey who did not like being in service. She had an affair with Major Charles Bryant while he was receiving treatment for a war injury at Downton Abbey. Mrs. Hughes caught them naked together in a storage room and Ethel was dismissed. Later she discovered she was pregnant by the Major. She wrote him several letters asking for his help but he failed to respond. Having few options, she returned to Downton Abbey and was assisted by Mrs. Hughes. The Major died in one of the last battles of World War I. In due time Ethel gave birth to Charles Parks. When the Major's parents visited Downton Abbey, Ethel, who was serving lunch, interrupted the meal to disclose her son's parentage. After initially rejecting Ethel's story, they sought to adopt and raise Charlie, giving him the benefit of their wealth. Ethel rejected this offer, wanting to keep the boy.

To make ends meet, Ethel became a prostitute. She encountered Isobel Crawley whose latest volunteer effort was helping prostitutes transition to other pursuits. Ethel, however, was reluctant to seek or accept assistance from Isobel.

When Charlie was almost two years old and Ethel was still struggling financially, she realized Charlie's life would be greatly enhanced if he lived with his fraternal grandparents because they could provide for him a comfortable life and save him from exposure to unsavory life styles. She thus relinquished the boy to them. Many tears were shed.

Ethel was offered a service job with a family who lived close to the Bryants. With the encouragement of Mrs. Bryant, Ethel accepted the job. Mrs. Bryant offered to enable Ethel to see Charlie on occasion. Ethel was very happy with this arrangement.

US LAW: A parent has certain rights in our law. These include determining how to provide for the child's emotional and physical well-being, selecting the child's religion, health and medical care, and schooling. When a custody battle occurs between a parent and a nonparent, the parent is always given preference absent a condition that renders the parent unable to provide for the child's well-being. Such conditions include an uncontrolled drug or alcohol addiction, an incurable and significant mental incompetency, and a debilitating chronic illness.

Courts have the authority to remove these parental rights both involuntarily and voluntarily. *Involuntary termination* occurs by court-order and may be the result of abuse or neglect of the child; inability of the parent to support the child financially, emotionally, and/or physically; alcohol or drug abuse; abandonment of the child; or a felony conviction. The requirements and procedures vary from state to state.

Voluntary termination occurs when a biological parent, acting on her or his own volition and not pursuant to court order, places the child for adoption. The parental rights are thereafter assigned to adoptive parents. Voluntary termination might occur because a parent decides s/he no longer wishes, for any of a variety or reasons, to be responsible for a child. Or like Ethel, parents without the financial means to provide for a child in the way they would like sometimes forfeit their rights to enable adoption by a family with better financial ability to provide for the child's needs. Such decisions are always difficult and poignant.

Note: In law, a child is entitled to a maximum of two parents. So, for a couple to adopt, the prior parent(s) must surrender their rights.

Once the parental rights have been surrendered, the child is available for adoption.

The laws and procedure to terminate parental rights vary by state. Generally, for a voluntarily relinquishment, a petition must be filed in the appropriate court. In an involuntary situation, the judge decides whether to grant the termination or not. The judge is bound to do, in the judge's opinion, whatever is in the best interests of the child

APPLICATION TO DA: In a heart-breaking scene, Ethel realized her son's paternal grandparents can provide for his needs and wants, and give him a life with the best chance to thrive. In an act of selfless love, she agreed to voluntarily forfeit her parental rights to enable the grandparents to adopt Charles. We are left to sympathize with Ethel's lot in life.

Chapter 15

Rights of a Fetus – O'brien and Cora

A FACTS: Sarah O'Brien, Cora's lady's maid, was a spiteful woman, seemingly enjoying watching others squirm who fall victim to her betrayals. Thus, it was perhaps not unexpected that she sought revenge even from her boss when O'Brien heard Cora and Violet talking about soliciting applications for a lady's maid. Believing her job was in jeopardy, she wanted retribution. Cora was pregnant and if the baby was a male, Downton Abbey would be saved from distant relatives. Everyone at Downton was keenly aware of the significance of that possibility. Spiteful O'Brien however was willing to risk the possibility of an in-house heir to settle the score as she saw it.

Thus, as Cora was bathing, O'Brien purposefully moved a bar of slippery soap from under the tub into Cora's walkway. Sure enough, as Cora exited the bath, her foot made contact with the soap, she slipped and fell, badly. Sadly, the incident resulted in a miscarriage. Turns out the fetus was a male. Alas, what might have been. And in the end O'Brien discovered it was not Cora who was seeking a new lady's maid but rather Violet. Nothing in the story line suggested O'Brien was wracked with guilt.

US LAW: Intentionally causing injury to another person is both a criminal and civil wrong. The crime is *assault*. The more serious the injury, the higher is the level of the crime and the more jail time the defendant faces. The civil wrong, is *battery*. The remedy for a civil wrong is compensation. The amount of money recovered by the plaintiff is dependent upon the seriousness of the injury, the amount of the doctor bills – both past and anticipated for the future, and the extent of the provable pain and anguish suffered by the injured party.

When the injury caused is death, the name of the lawsuit is *wrongful death*, meaning plaintiff claims that someone died due to the legal fault of another person. In the factual situation involving Cora and O'Brien, the life of the fetus was terminated. This raises the question - Does a fetus have a right to sue for wrongful death? The answer depends on the state in which the injury occurred as the states are divided on this issue. Approximately two-thirds permit a wrongful death claim where a fetus is extinguished. However, in many of those states the fetus must have reached a specified point of development before its death can be compensated. In some states a fetus not yet born cannot claim compensation. In others, viability (ability to survive outside the mother's womb) with or without aid, is the test, and a few states require that the fetus be *quick*, meaning that the mother is able to feel the fetus moving inside her.

Approximately one-third of the states either prohibit lawsuits by fetuses or have not addressed the issue.

People who are opposed to abortion would advocate for giving the fetus a right to sue because such recognition of the fetus as a being enhances the argument that a fetus should be protected beginning at conception, rendering abortion the equivalent of murder.

APPLICATION TO DA: O'Brien's actions were clearly mean-spirited and illegal. The soap incident would qualify as both criminal assault and the civil wrong of battery. However, Cora was unaware of Obrien's culpability in the slip and fall incident and so would not know to accuse her. Additionally, there would be little purpose in Cora suing O'Brien since O'Brien, as a servant, likely has little money. She may be *judgment-proof*, meaning she does not have the means to satisfy a judgment that might be entered against her. For that same reason, the issue of whether the fetus can sue is of intellectual interest only. The answer would depend on the state in which the miscarriage occurs.

Chapter 16

Medical Privacy – Lady Sybil and Dr. Ryder

DA FACTS: Mathew and Mary were both concerned that Mary had not become pregnant. Both, without the other's knowledge, visited Dr. Ryder, a fertility physician. While there, he inquired whether Mary had sought treatment from him. The doctor replied that he could not answer due to patient confidentiality.

ADDITIONAL DA FACTS: Something went wrong with Lady Sybil's pregnancy. Robert called the country doctor, Dr. Clarkson, who diagnosed the problem as Preeclampsia. The doctor recommended Sybil go to the hospital right away for an emergency C-section. Cora agreed but Lord Grantham was not convinced of the diagnosis. He summoned Dr. Philip Tapsell, a specialist from London. Both Dr. Tapsell and Lord Grantham believed that taking Sybil to the village hospital for a Caesarean section would be far too risky to Sybil and the baby.

There ensued much discussion and argument about the proper treatment. Present in the bedroom during the discussions were Cora and Robert, Sybil's husband Branson, and her sisters, Mary and Edith.

US LAW: Federal law imposes on doctors a strict duty to maintain clients' health information as confidential. The Health Insurance Portability and Accountability Act of 1996, known by the acronym HIPPA, contains a privacy rule that establishes national standards to protect from disclosure individuals' medical records and other personal health information. The Act requires appropriate safeguards by doctors and others to protect the privacy of personal health information, and sets limits and conditions on the uses and disclosures that may be made without patient authorization.

However, a medical provider may speak to certain individuals about a patient under specified circumstances. If a patient is unconscious or incapacitated, a health care provider can share the patient's information with family or friends, as long as the physician determines, based on professional judgment, that disclosure is in the best interest of the patient. Further, under an emergency situation, the doctor may discuss the condition of the patient.

APPLICATION TO DA: Dr. Ryder acted appropriately by declining to answer Mathew's question about whether Mary had visited the fertility doctor. The duty of confidentiality applies even to the fact of whether a patient has sought treatment by a doctor, and even to a spouse.

Concerning Lady Sybil, given her condition in the birthing room, she would likely be considered incapacitated. Further, the facts suggest an emergency situation. Therefore, the doctors' discussions of her condition and treatment recommendations with her parents, husband and sisters did not violate privacy laws. Thus, the doctors would not have been liable under HIPPA for unauthorized disclosure of Sybil's condition.

Chapter 17

Nuremberg Laws – Rose and Atticus

FACTS: *(Note: This is the second of the two chapters in which law from a country other than the United States is discussed.)* Lovely Lady Rose MacClare, cousin to the Crawleys, married the debonair Atticus Aldridge. He is Jewish, as are both his parents. Atticus' ancestors fled pogroms in Russia 60 years earlier. Lord Sinderby, Atticus' dad, is distraught that his son is marrying outside the Jewish faith.

While Rose had no Jewish blood, Cora's father was Jewish, rendering Cora in many circles half-Jewish, making her daughters quarter-Jewish. Due to that connection, Robert and Cora had no objection to Rose's marriage to Atticus.

RELEVANT LAW: The Nuremberg Laws of Hitler's Germany imposed severe restrictions on German Jews. These laws, announced on September 15, 1935, reinforced pronouncements and practices adopted by Germany prior to that date. Among other restrictions, Jews were prohibited from marrying or having sexual relations with persons of "German or related blood." Violation of this prohibition constituted a crime, titled Racial infamy.

Other restrictions barred Jews from working for the government; teaching as faculty at colleges; attending German schools; taking university entrance exams; practicing dentistry; continuing German citizenship; acting in plays; inheriting farmland; working for newspapers or magazines; holding public office;

obtaining national health insurance; working at a stock exchange; continuing membership in civic associations; going to theaters, public swimming pools or resorts; and hoisting the German flag.

Non-Jews were forbidden to shop at Jewish-owned stores and were required to cancel credit accounts with them. Likewise, non-Jews were forbidden to enter cafes and restaurants frequented by Jews. As a result, signs saying "Jews Unwelcome" proliferated.

The Nuremberg Laws defined a Jew not based on religious beliefs but rather ancestry. People with three or four Jewish grandparents were defined as Jewish regardless of their religious affiliation. Even people with the requisite number of Jewish grandparents who had converted to Christianity were defined as Jews.

Ultimately, the German Reich exterminated six million Jews and other segments of society deemed "undesirable" by Hitler, the German Chancellor, including the disabled, mentally ill, gypsies, the homeless, and others.

APPLICATION TO DA: In the early years of Hitler's rule, Germany sought to befriend Britain seeing possibilities for a strategic alliance. The United Kingdom was not a willing partner, totally changing Hitler's attitude toward the country. England was able to repel Germany's aerial assault, causing Hitler to postpone a planned invasion. Ultimately, British forces contributed greatly to the defeat of Germany. Therefore, while the war significantly disrupted lives throughout Europe, the Nazi's repressive laws did not apply in England. Thus, the legality of Rose and Atticus' union was not impacted by the Nuremberg Laws.

Note: Assuming Cora's father's parents were both Jewish, Cora would still not have been considered Jewish in Nazi Germany because neither of her mother's parents was Jewish. So the maximum number of Jewish grandparents she had was two, below the dreaded qualifying three.

Business Law

Chapter 18

Americans with Disabilities Act – Mr. Bates

DA FACTS: Mr. Bates came to Downton Abbey at the invitation of Robert Crawley for the purpose of serving as the Earl's valet. The job responsibilities included preparing the clothing Robert will wear, brushing and cleaning it, polishing boots, assisting in dressing him, readying gloves and hat, tidying the dressing room, ensuring toiletries were in their proper place and ready for use, and receiving and executing orders for the rest of the day. The job at Downton Abbey necessitated trips up and down stairs that went from the lower level where the servants gather, work and eat, to the main level of the mansion, and upstairs to the master bedroom and dressing area. The job demanded some level of agility.

As was known to Robert, Mr. Bates' leg was injured during the Boer Wars while Bates served as batman (a soldier assigned to a military officer as a servant) to Lord Grantham. As a result, Bates walked with a limp and a cane. When he first came to Downton Abbey, the other servants expressed concern that he would not be able to fulfill the requirements of the job. Thomas Barrow, then footman, had sought the valet position and was disappointed he was not promoted. He was particularly impatient with Mr. Bates' limitations, few though they were.

US LAW: Leading up to the early 1990's, the United States observed that many people with disabilities, were quite able to work but were nonetheless denied jobs, in large part because of stereotypes about handicaps and related medical needs. To enable disabled would-be workers to overcome the inaccurate stigmas, Congress passed the Americans with Disabilities Act. It outlaws discrimination against workers who, despite disabilities, are able to perform the *essential functions of a job* (the core, fundamental duties of a position).

APPLICATION TO DA: While Mr. Bates clearly suffered from a leg injury that inhibited him from walking normally and from other physical activities such as running, he was able to perform the tasks required of a valet. Therefore, it would be illegal for the Crawleys to terminate Bates because of his disability.

Chapter 19

Bankruptcy – Robert

A FACTS: Against his broker's advice, Lord Grantham invested the bulk of his wife's inheritance in one Canadian railway company's stock, Grand Trunk Railway[3]. Unfortunately, the railroad went bankrupt. The earl was stunned because "everyone knew" the Canadian railroads were a "surefire" investment.

US LAW: Bankruptcy is the process of reducing, eliminating or restructuring debts of a company or person whose credit is overextended and who is unable to pay obligations within the foreseeable future. Bankruptcy is usually triggered by cash flow problems and related financial distress.

The laws that define the process to go bankrupt are federal laws adopted by Congress. The framers of the United States Constitution granted to Congress the power to establish bankruptcy laws so they would be uniform throughout the fifty states. Bankruptcy proceedings are litigated in a specially constituted court – the United States Bankruptcy Court.

The bankruptcy laws provide several types of bankruptcy, embodied in chapters of the bankruptcy law. Which type is used in a given case depends on

---

3 This is one of numerous references where Downton Abbey storylines overlap with historical occurrences. The Grand Trunk Railway was a major Canadian railroad company that experienced significant financial troubles due to inflated construction costs, competition from shipping and American railroads, overestimated revenues, and inadequate initial capitalization.

whether the bankrupt (the party unable to pay debts) is an individual, a business, a governmental entity, or a farmer.

For example, a business pursuing bankruptcy but seeking to remain operational would likely use *Chapter 11* which provides many possibilities for reorganizing debt. The result is typically payment of some part of the debt, cancellation of some obligations, and restructuring of the balance, meaning a significant modification of the terms of the financial obligations. The upshot is the debt load is lessened so the debtor has a realistic chance of paying the remaining commitment.

Another type of bankruptcy is called *Chapter 7*, which involves liquidation of a company, meaning it ceases operations and goes out of business. In this type of bankruptcy, the court appoints a *trustee* whose function is to liquidate (sell) the company's assets and then apply the money to pay the debt. If the amount of the debt exceeds the proceeds from the sale, the remaining unpaid debts that are not secured (no collateral) are extinguished, meaning the creditor takes the loss and the debtor does not have to pay. With secured debt, the creditor can repossess the property that serves as collateral, sell it, and apply the proceeds to the debt.

Certain types of debt are not usually eliminated in bankruptcy. Instead, they remain an obligation of the bankrupt business or individual even after the proceedings are complete. For a company, these include recent tax obligations. For individuals, other debts not extinguished include child support, restitution imposed in criminal cases, a money judgment resulting from an accident caused by driving while intoxicated, and student loans.

From an investment vantage point, a prudent person in Lord Grantham's circumstance with a significant amount of money to invest would have consulted an investment advisor. That person would no doubt have recommended that Robert diversify his holdings. Rather than put all the money in one company, a much safer option is to buy other stocks, perhaps acquire some government notes and bonds, save some cash for a rainy day, and consider other types of investments as well. If one of the investments fails, the balance of the portfolio would remain intact.

APPLICATION TO DA: The Grand Truck Railway likely utilized Chapter 7 total liquidation, rendering the Earl's investment in the company worth close to zero. Since he had not diversified, virtually of the money was dissipated. A sad day in the Crawley household.

Chapter 20

Contracts: Condition Precedent – Joseph Molesley

FACTS: Molesley fell on hard times and was working at a grocery store delivering food. At Downton Abbey, it appeared that Alfred Nugent, a footman, would be leaving for London to pursue his dream of becoming a chef. Carson informed Molesley of the possible opening and offered the position to Molesley should it materialize. However, Alfred's application to the cooking school was initially rejected and so he had no immediate intention to leave the estate.

US LAW: Offers may be subject to a *condition precedent*, a legal term meaning an event that must occur before an offer is effective. If the event does not occur, the offer has no legal effect and does not give rise to a contract.

APPLICATION TO DA: Carson's offer to Molesley was subject to a condition precedent – Alfred leaving Downton's employ. Had Alfred not left, there would be no opening and thus no effective offer to hire Molesley. Since the condition precedent did not initially occur, there is no effective offer of employment for Molesley to accept or reject.

Chapter 21

Contracts: Exculpatory Clauses – Titanic Passengers

DA FACTS: James Crawley, Robert Crawley's cousin, and Patrick Crawley, fiancé of Mary Crawley, were passengers aboard the Titanic. Sadly, they both drowned when the great ship sank.

To board the Titanic, passengers needed a ticket. On the ticket was a *waiver of liability*, verbiage that purportedly relieved the owners of the ship from legal responsibility if anyone was injured or killed while at sea. Since the ship was touted as unsinkable, it is doubtful that any passengers gave much thought to the waiver.

A typical waiver of liability reads as follows:

"I, for myself, my heirs, personal representatives or assigns, do hereby release, waive and discharge _(add company name here)_ their officers, agents, representatives, employees from liability for any and all claims including the negligence of the said company and its staff, resulting in personal injury, accidents or illnesses (including death),

and property loss arising from, but not limited to, (fill in the type of business or the service the company provides)"

US LAW: The term for this type of contract provision is *exculpatory clause*; it seeks to exculpate, meaning free, a party from liability. The enforceability of these provisions depends on the state in which the parties reside. As a general rule, these clauses are not favored by the law. Some states refuse to enforce them as contrary to public policy. In other words, those states are committed to the policy that if a business or person acts carelessly and causes injury as a result, that person or business should be liable for the consequences.

Some states will enforce exculpatory clauses with certain exceptions. One is *gross negligence*, meaning carelessness to a significant degree, extreme or very blameworthy. In those states, an exculpatory clause would not be effective against a defendant who is grossly negligent. Also, many states will decline to enforce a waiver of liability if the injury was caused by negligence, and the contract term fails to include the word "negligence" among the circumstances for which a party is excused from liability.

Most states that enforce these clauses require that the wording be clear, meaning easily understood and not obfuscated by legalese. Another requirement is that the provision be *conspicuous*, meaning noticeable and difficult to overlook, as opposed to small print, lost in the middle of a lengthy agreement, or written in ink so light the clause is hard to see or read.

APPLICATION TO DA: To determine the enforceability of the Titanic's exculpatory clause, a court would have to review the relevant state's concerning liability waivers. All cases against the owners of the Titanic were eventually settled so a judicial determination of the enforceability of the clause was not required or made. However, the owners no doubt utilized the clause to obtain bargaining power in the settlement negotiations, enabling them to resolve the cases for less than might have occurred had the tickets not included an exculpatory clause.

Chapter 22

Contract Law: Restaurant Reservations – Anna and Mr. Bates

FACTS: Following the rape of Anna, she and Mr. Bates decided to make new and happy memories. In furtherance of that goal, they arranged to dine at an upscale restaurant. When they arrived, the condescending maitre d' claimed he could not find their reservation, presumably because they were of service status. Fortunately, Cora also was dining there with members of a society charity organization. Upon seeing Anna and Bates, Cora approached and greeted them, and insisted that the maître d' seat the couple.

US LAW: An interesting question arises whether the restaurant would have been liable for breach of contract if the maître d' had not relented on providing a table for Anna and Bates. This is a question that has vexed restaurants because would-be diners with reservations not infrequently are no-shows. Therefore, restaurants, like other businesses, not infrequently overbook. If everyone with a reservation comes, the eatery will be unable to accommodate them all in a timely fashion.

When making a restaurant reservation, the customer typically inquires whether a table for a certain number of people is available at a given time. In response, the restaurant indicates yes or no, or provides proposed alternative times. The caller may then indicate a willingness to dine at the time proposed; that is an acceptance. Presumably, both parties are serious about the arrangement – the restaurant is in business to provide food to the public for a profit, and the caller is intending to eat at the restaurant on the date and time indicated. It appears a contract exists.

If so, the restaurant will be in *breach* (violation) if it fails to provide a table at the designated time, or within a reasonable amount of time thereafter. Likewise, if a contract exists, guests who do not show will be in breach.

Industry custom seems to excuse a would-be guest who fails to show, and therefore might likewise excuse a restaurant that fails to provide a table to a guest with reservations. Given the limited loss that the parties likely experience, few lawsuits have been pursued so the applicable law is not well-developed or clear.

However, if the refusal of a restaurant to honor a reservation is based on the would-be guests being in a protected class – such as race, color, religion, national origin, disability, gender, and in some locations, sexual orientation – the restaurant would be liable for violation of civil rights laws.

APPLICATION TO DA: Given the limited law supporting a restaurant reservation as a contract, it is hard to predict if the restaurant would face liability had it refused to seat Anna and Bates, and had they wished to press the issue. Concerning a possible civil rights claim, the restaurant would not be liable even if the refusal was based on Anna and Bates status since servants are not a protected class. Fortunately for the couple, Cora happened upon the scene at the critical moment.

Chapter 23

Contracts: Revocation of an Offer – Mr. Carson and Joseph Molesley

A FACTS:[4] Joseph Molesley fell on hard times and was was delivering groceries for a living. At Downton Abbey, it appeared that Alfred Nugent, a footman, would be leaving for London to pursue his dream of becoming a chef. Carson informed Molesley of the possible opening and offered the position to Molesley should it materialize. In doing so, Carson believed he was doing Molesley a major favor. However, Molesley fancied himself a valet or butler, and was not thrilled about the footman position. He told Carson he would think about it. Carson felt rebuffed, and when Molesley later advised Carson he wished to accept the position, Carson informed Molesley the offer was no longer open.

Note: When Alfred left, Mrs. Hughes and Mrs. Patmore advocated for Molesley. They were convincing, and Carson begrudgingly agreed to rehire Molesley.

US LAW: A *contract* is an agreement between two or more parties that is enforceable in court. To establish the existence of a contract, evidence must exist of both parties' intent to form an agreement. That evidence is typically embodied in an *offer* and an *acceptance*. An offer is a proposal to give or do

---
4 This situation is also examined from a different legal perspective in Chapter 20.

something of value in exchange for the same. The person making the offer is called the *offeror*. The person to whom an offer is made is called the *offeree*. An *acceptance* is a response by the offeree indicating unequivocal agreement to the terms of an offer.

As a general rule, an offeror can withdraw the offer anytime before acceptance, but not after.

APPLICATION TO DA: Carson was bound when Molesley advised Carson that Molesely wished to accept the position. This is so because Molesley's acceptance occurred before Carson sought to withdraw the offer.

Chapter 24

Employment: Interview Questions – Phyllis Baxter

FACTS: Lady Grantham hired Miss Baxter as her lady's maid on the recommendation of Thomas Barrow. Neither Baxter nor Barrow disclosed that Baxter had spent three years in prison for stealing from a previous employer. Nor did Cora inquire.

US LAW: There are numerous laws that restrict the questions that an employer can ask an applicant concerning prior criminal conduct. One such rule prevents an employer from inquiring about arrests, as opposed to convictions. The fact of an arrest does not establish that criminal conduct occurred.

Most state laws restrict questions about convictions to those involving crimes that are job-related. Thus, a hotel hiring a driver for a hospitality van could inquire about prior driving while intoxicated convictions. The same hotel hiring a laundry worker could not. Some states restrict questions of convictions to those occurring within ten years of the job interview.

If a person with a conviction is not offered the job, some states entitle the applicant, upon request, to a written explanation why. This helps to ensure both that employers do not illegally discriminate on the basis of an unrelated conviction, and qualified ex-offenders are evaluated on their merits.

An issue that has received much attention in the last several years is widely known as "ban the box" (proposed removal from employment applications of the question about prior criminal convictions) or "fair-chance policy". This effort prevents employers from inquiring about prior criminal convictions until after an initial interview. The goal is for employers to consider candidates' qualifications without the immediate stigma of a conviction record. Momentum grew quickly for this initiative resulting in at least 26 states, Washington DC, and more than 100 cities adopting variations of the ban-the-box rule.

APPLICATION TO DA: Hiring at Downton Abbey was rather informal, with friends or relatives of current servants being given the benefit of the doubt. In hiring Baxter, Cora relied heavily on Tom's recommendation. Had Cora conducted a more formal application process, she could have asked about convictions for stealing since a lady's maid has significant access to the personal effects of her employer. In many states and cities, Lady Grantham would not have been able to inquire about Miss Baxter's criminal record until after the first interview due to ban-the-box laws. Once the information came to light, Cora could consider it in making the hiring decision.

Chapter 25

Employment: Letters of Recommendation – Edna Braithwaite

A FACTS: In a drunken stupor, Branson had a sexual encounter with lady's maid Edna Braithwaite. Thereafter she threatened Tom that she may be pregnant and demanded to know if he would marry her if she was with child. Tom was disappointed with himself and, still in deep mourning for Sybil, was distraught about the situation. He confided in Mrs. Hughes who confronted Edna with a book on birth control Mrs. Hughes found hidden in Edna's room. The book was evidence that Edna took precautions to avoid getting pregnant. The head housekeeper ordered Edna to resign and foreclosed any further claims against Branson by telling Edna, "If you want a reference or another job during your natural lifetime, you'll hold your tongue!"

US LAW: Employers are often asked to provide letters of recommendation for employees. There is no legal duty that requires an employer to provide such a letter. If given, the communication typically includes both facts and opinions. Employers writing such letters want to avoid liability for *defamation*, the legal wrong of relaying untruthful statements about a person that harms that person's reputation. The law of defamation provides a *qualified privilege* when an employer writes a letter of recommendation, meaning an employer will not be liable for defamation provided the letter is not knowingly false, opinions are based on substantiated facts, and the communication is disclosed only to those with a reason to know, such as a potential new employer.

APPLICATION TO DA: If Mrs. Hughes provided a letter of recommendation that suggested Edna attempted to mislead and blackmail one of her employers, that information would be truthful. Therefore, if Edna were to sue for defamation, her case would not be successful.

Chapter 26

Negligence: Respondeat Superior – Titanic

DA FACTS: As the series begins, Mary was engaged to Patrick Crawley. Sadly, he and his father James were passengers on the ill-fated Titanic. Like so many passengers, they went down with the ship, despite the owner's boasting that the craft was unsinkable. While the Downton Abbey series does not dwell on the circumstances of the ship's demise, the facts are well-documented in history. The great vessel sank four days into her maiden voyage from Southampton, England to New York City. It was the largest passenger liner in service at the time, and was carrying approximately 2,224 passengers. Alas, on April 14, 1912 it struck an iceberg in the north Atlantic Ocean, triggering events that caused the death of 1,517 people.

Numerous circumstances contributed to the loss of life. The ship's captain had received several iceberg warnings that day from other ships in the area but he failed to reduce the Titanic's speed or take other indicated precautions. Neither the crew nor the passengers had been properly trained in emergency procedures or lifeboat evacuations.

As the exodus unfolded, lifeboats were lowered into the water with significantly less people than the boats' maximum capacity, resulting in many less passengers than possible escaping death by drowning. Also, the lifeboats were not equipped with emergency supplies resulting in many people dying of hypothermia while waiting on the small boats for rescue ships.

US LAW: At all times, people and businesses are required by law to act carefully to avoid foreseeable harm to others. Failure to exercise a reasonable degree of caution in circumstances where injury can be foreseen constitutes *negligence*, meaning carelessness. A person who acts negligently is liable to anyone injured thereby.

When an employee is negligent in the performance of his official duties, the employer is liable for resulting injuries. This imposition of liability is based on the legal principle of *respondeat superior*, meaning the boss responds in law for the wrongdoing of the worker. While this may at first blush seem unfair, the rule is intended to encourage employers to hire carefully, train employees well, and supervise them reasonably closely on an ongoing basis.

APPLICATION TO DA: The owner of the Titanic, White Star Line, would be liable for negligence based on respondeat superior. That company hired the captain. His failure to slow the ship amid iceberg sightings was negligent. Failure to train the crew and instruct passengers on evacuation procedures complicated and slowed the process of moving passengers into lifeboats, and constituted negligence. Had proper training been provided, the many unfilled seats in the lifeboats might have been filled. Unlike those hapless passengers who drowned on the ship's deck, everyone in a lifeboat at least had a chance to survive. Failure to stock the dinghies with emergency provisions was also negligent and contributed to the deaths of many before their lifeboat was safely recovered.

Hundreds of survivors and also family members of the deceased together sued the White Star Line seeking more than $16 million in damages to cover loss of life, loss of property, and compensation for injuries and emotional scars from the evacuation. The company that owned the ship denied liability claiming the accident was not foreseeable, and the number of lifeboats satisfied English law at the time.

In the end, the ship's owners settled the case for $664,000, which was divided among the claimants. As a result of various investigations of the ship sinking, a convention (meeting of interested parties to review relevant law), known as SOLAS (Safety of Life at Sea), was held by maritime companies. New safety precautions for passenger ships were adopted. Those requirements included sufficient lifeboat capacity for all passengers and crew.

Mandates continue to be added and now include enclosed lifeboats so if they tip, passengers are protected from the water. These were portrayed in the movie Captain Phillips. Other needed equipment on board and required protocols include fire and smoke detection devices, automatic sprinkler systems, fire training, fire and lifeboat drills for the crew, lifeboat instruction for passengers, electronic safety gear, and navigational equipment.

Chapter 27

Partnerships – Mathew and Robert

A FACTS: Mathew used his inheritance from Lavinia's father to help the financial circumstances of Downton Abbey. In exchange for this investment, Mathew became a partner with Robert in managing the estate. The two initially disagreed on numerous operational issues. Mathew was more efficient and financially focused than Robert. Mathew sought to institute new procedures, and Robert was committed to the traditional ways of running the mansion.

Mathew solicited Tom to help resolve the disagreements. Together they convinced Robert that changes were necessary.

US LAW: When parties become business partners, they should create a written partnership agreement that clearly identifies each partner's rights and responsibilities. The agreement will define the parties' relationship and should thereby eliminate many disagreements since the entitlements and duties are addressed and resolved in the writing. If the partners do not develop a partnership contract, disputes are by law resolved by application of state partnership law. These laws "fill in the blanks," meaning provide terms of partners' relationship when a written agreement is nonexistent or is silent on the matter causing dissention.

Most state partnership laws provide that each partner's vote is weighted equally, and partners can act only by majority vote. With a two partner arrangement, such as Robert and Mathew have, the necessary majority vote requires both to agree.

APPLICATION TO DA: Mathew wanted Downton Abbey to expand into new pursuits, and Robert was not agreeable. Mathew would lack the necessary authority to take unilateral action in furtherance of his vision. Fortunately, Tom and Mathew were able to convince Robert of the correctness of their position. Having secured Robert's consent, Mathew had the necessary vote to proceed with his plans.

Chapter 28

Warranties – Mr. Bates

FACTS: Mr. Bates, whose leg was injured during the Boers Wars leaving him with a limp, saw an ad for a "limp corrector" from a shop that specializes in artificial limbs, braces and related items. He visited the store to learn more about the product. It looked like a metal brace big enough to run the full length of a leg.

Bates purchased one and took it back to Downton to try. Turns out it was very painful and a total failure as a mechanism to alleviate his handicap. Disappointed, he tossed it in a pond in Carson's presence, both bidding it "good riddance."

US LAW: The law imposes on every sale of goods an *implied warranty* (imposed by law, not verbalized or written) that the goods are *merchantable*, meaning fit for their ordinary purpose. Thus, a limp corrector should be capable of correcting limps. If not, it violates the warranty. The buyer would be entitled to reimbursement of the purchase price and compensation for any injuries suffered.

Another warranty arises when a seller makes a statement about the performance potential of a good. Unlike an *implied warranty*, which arises even without the parties addressing it, a verbalized guarantee is an *express warranty*, meaning a guarantee that is stated or written. By calling the apparatus a limp corrector, the seller is representing that the metal contraption is capable of eliminating a limp. If the product is not up to the task, the warranty is *breached*, meaning violated.

APPLICATION TO DA: Sadly for Mr. Bates, the limp corrector did not fulfill the promise of its name. Thus, the implied warranty of merchantability as well as the express warranty created by the device's description were both breached. Bates would be entitled to return of the money he paid for the device, plus compensation for any injuries the device might have caused him. While he did experience some pain, his use of the apparatus was short-lived so the discomfort was of very limited duration and so Bates would garner little from a lawsuit.

Criminal Law – Specific Crimes

Chapter 29

Elements of a Crime – Investigator Vyner

A FACTS: Investigator Vyner came to Downton Abbey on several occasions to investigate the murder of Mr. Green and question people of interest. Among those the officer interrogated were Mary and Mr. Bates, both of whom arguably have a *motive* (a reason for engaging in certain conduct) for the murder. Bates' motive would have been revenge. And we know that Bates would be only too happy to get even. Anna too might have been inclined to kill Green because if he was dead, she would not need to fear another sexual assault by him.

US LAW: Every crime has two elements:

1. A wrongful act, such as taking another person's life
2. A criminal mental state, which is usually interpreted as *intentionally*, meaning the defendant's conscious objective was to engage the prohibited *act*.

This means the defendant knew what he was doing when he did it, and by so acting an inference arises that defendant intended the consequences of his actions.

APPLICATION TO DA: Although Mary, Anna and Bates all had a motive to commit the homicide, that is not a necessary component of a crime. All the prosecutor must prove is that a specific person intentionally killed Green. The existence of a motive is not necessary for a conviction. Motive, however, often renders a jury more willing to find a defendant guilty. This is so because the motive provides an explanation for why the defendant would have carried out the illegal act.

Motive however can be misleading. Although Mary, Anna and Bates each had motive to dislike Green intensely, apparently none of them committed his murder.

Chapter 30

Arson – Branson

DA FACTS: In uprisings against the English aristocracy in colonial Ireland, Branson sided with rebels. He participated in a protest that unexpectedly turned violent when demonstrators burned the Irish home of an English official.

US LAW: Arson is the crime of intentionally damaging another's property by starting a fire or causing an explosion. *Degreeing factors* (circumstances that elevate the seriousness of the crime) include burning a building or car (as opposed to other property), the presence of people inside a burned building, and use of an incendiary device.

APPLICATION TO DA: Whoever started the fire at the aristocrat's home is guilty of arson. The charge will be a *felony* (a more serious crime for which the maximum jail time exceeds one year) because at least one degreeing factor was present – a building (the house) was the target of the fire.

Chapter 31

Bribery – Harold Levinson

***D*A FACTS:** Lady Cora Grantham's brother, Harold Levinson, lived in the United States. He wrote to Lord Grantham informing the Earl that he, Cora's brother, was having legal troubles due to investments that were related to the Teapot Dome scandal. At Levinson's request, Lord Grantham, an honorable brother-in-law, left for America to assist. The details of Levinson's involvement with the scandal are not disclosed. For an educated guess, a background about the scandal is necessary.

The events were related to the use of oil to fuel the country's fleet of navy ships. Until approximately 1909, the ships ran on coal. Navy administrators determined that petroleum-run fleets would be more efficient both because coaling stations would no longer be required, and the boats could go farther on oil than coal. As the transition progressed, Navy administrators were concerned that access to oil might be limited. Therefore, Congress designated as "naval petroleum reserves" three federally owned land parcels known for high oil deposits. These became exempt from drilling unless a national emergency necessitated their use. One of the reserves was located in a place named for an unusual rock formation – Teapot Dome. (A dome is a geological formation that traps oil underground between impervious layers of rock, causing the upper layer to bend upward to form a dome).

Men in the oil business recognized the value of the designated lands and resented being unable to drill on them. President Harding's Secretary of the Interior, Albert Bacon Fall, convinced Harding to transfer control of the reserves to Fall's Department. Fall then made secret deals with two oilmen, permitting them to drill in return for handsome bribes. Independent oilmen began to raise questions when they saw trucks hauling drilling equipment on the reserves. Following a Senate investigation, Fall was tried and convicted of accepting bribes. He was sentenced to a year in jail and was fined $100,000, a lot of money in 1920's dollars. He was the first cabinet-level officer in American history to go to jail for crimes committed while in office.

US LAW: Bribery is a crime consisting of offering, giving, receiving or soliciting something of value for the purpose of influencing the action of officials in the discharge of their public or legal duties. The result is a betrayal by the official of his responsibilities. All states have bribery laws that prohibit both the government official from accepting the bribe and any person from offering a bribe.

APPLICATION TO DA: Viewers do not become privy to the details of Levinson's troubles surrounding the Teapot Dome scandal. If fictionally he was one of the oilmen who gave Fall money in exchange for drilling rights, he would be guilty of bribery and would face potential jail time and sizable fines.

Chapter 32

Trespass and Burglary – Terence Sampson

DA FACTS: Terence Sampson was an acquaintance of Robert's from his gentlemen's club. Sampson escorted Rosamund Painswick to the pre-party for Rose MacClare's coming out. He then joined Rose and Freda Dudley Ward at the Embassy Club. Lady Freda was the paramour of the Prince of Wales who became King Edward VIII. However, he chose to renounce the crown in less than a year rather than end his relationship with Ms. Ward. Rose, in her naiveté, disclosed the existence of a compromising letter in Lady Freda's purse from the then Prince. Sampson, cad that he is, secretly removed the letter from Lady Freda's purse. The note had the potential of greatly embarrassing the Prince.

When Lady Freda informed Rose that the letter is missing, Rose suspected Sampson. She spoke to Robert who no doubt correctly surmised that Sampson intended to profit from the note, either by blackmailing Mrs. Ward or selling the letter to foreign newspapers. Robert and Rose hatched a plan. Robert occupied Sampson with a card game while Rose and Mary, using a forged letter to gain entry past a doorman, entered Sampson's flat, and prowled around. Alas, they did not find the letter.

US LAW: The crime of *trespass* consists of entering or remaining unlawfully on premises. The crime of *burglary* consists of the crime of trespass plus the intention to commit a crime inside or on the premises. The crime intended is typically theft but could also be rape, criminal mischief (property damage), assault, or any other crime.

APPLICATION TO DA: Rose and Mary entered Sampson's living quarters under false pretenses and without actual permission. This constitutes the crime of trespass. They would have taken the subject letter had they found it. That would have constituted the crime of stealing, also called *larceny*. Since Rose and Mary committed trespass with the intent to commit a crime, it appears (wrongly as will be explained) that they also committed burglary.

Note: Burglary does not require the actual commission of the crime intended. The mere intent to commit the crime inside the area trespassed is sufficient.

There is however another interesting twist to these facts. The letter did not belong to Sampson. Is it a crime to take something that another person possesses illegally? Stealing consists of wrongfully taking property from its "owner." That word is defined as any person who has a right of possession superior to that of the burglar. Since Sampson apparently stole the letter, he had no right of possession. Therefore, while Rose and Mary committed trespass by entering Sampson's property without permission, Sampson had no right to the letter and so Mary and Rose's intention to remove it was not criminal. Their crime therefore was limited to trespass.

Chapter 33

Conspiracy – Durant and Craig

DA FACTS: Mr. Bates was sent to prison for the murder of his wife. Fortunately, exculpatory evidence was discovered and he was released. While in custody, one of the guards, Durant, and Bates' cellmate, Craig, were working together to sell illegal drugs behind bars. Durant would secure the drugs and bring them into the prison. Craig's role was to sell the contraband to inmates.

US LAW: The crime of conspiracy consists of an agreement between two or more people to commit a crime, any crime, together. To prove a conspiracy, evidence is required of an overt act committed by at least one of the conspirators and done in furtherance of the illegal plan. A mere association between two persons planning a crime does not alone amount to conspiracy. To prove the crime of conspiracy, a prosecutor must establish the following facts: 1) an intent to commit a crime with the assistance of another; 2) an agreement between two or more parties to commit a crime together; and 3) the commission of that overt act in furtherance of the conspiracy by at least one of the conspirators.

APPLICATION TO DA: The activities of Durant and Craig, together selling illegal drugs to the prison population, is a conspiracy. Possessing or selling illegal drugs is criminal. Likewise, introducing into a prison population any *contraband* (goods that are illegal to possess), is the crime of possession of prison contraband.

Durant and Craig's agreement to work together to sell unlawful drugs in the prison, coupled with the overt acts of Durant providing the drugs to Craig, and Craig peddling them to fellow prisoners, constitutes the conspiracy.

Chapter 34

Endangering the Welfare of a Child – Nanny West

A FACTS: Nanny West was hired to be the governess and nanny for George Crawley, son of Mary and Mathew, and also for Sybbie Branson, daughter of Sybil and Branson. West made an enemy of Thomas, not a wise a move given his fearless mean streak. The bad blood began when she was walking Sybbie in a baby buggy, known in England as a pram. As Thomas approached them, West ordered him not to touch the baby. He took umbrage.

Thomas observed an incident where West withheld an egg from Sybbie after the baby showed a liking for that food. West later gave Thomas orders but he ignored her. In a petty row sure to irk Thomas, West claimed her rank was higher than his. When dissed, Thomas would get even. He alleged to Cora that West was leaving the children unsupervised. Based on this information, Cora investigated and overheard West speaking abusively to little Sybbie, calling her a "wicked little crossbreed."

Cora terminated the nanny immediately and gave her only until the next morning to pack her bags and leave. In the meantime, Cora ordered that West not be left alone with the children. West tried to defend herself by claiming she was only joking, but not surprisingly, any humor was lost on Cora. Instead, Cora retorted that West's "values have no place in a civilized home."

US LAW: A crime exists called *Endangering the welfare of a child*. While the elements vary from state to state, generally the crime is committed by engaging in conduct towards a young person in a way likely to injure his/her physical, mental or moral wellbeing.

APPLICATION TO DA: Had Sybbie been older and understood the meaning of West's words, her mental welfare and self-image would likely have been impaired. However, given the baby's tender age, we do not know if she absorbed the meaning of West's nasty comments.

There is no evidence of physical abuse of the children by West. Actual harm is not necessary in most states for commission of the crime. It is sufficient that a defendant acts in a manner likely to result in harm to a child. While the nanny's conduct was despicable, assuming Sybbie was too young to understand West's comments, her behavior likely does not rise to the level of the crime of endangering the welfare of a minor.

Chapter 35

Extortion and Coercion – Vera Bates

DA FACTS: Mr. Bates' estranged wife Vera was a nasty woman. Love between them faded long ago. She seemingly found joy in the discomfort of others. Unfortunately for Anna and Bates, Vera's prime target was Mr. Bates. In one circumstance, Vera was hired as a member of the household staff of the Marquess of Flintshire. Vera secured the job by misusing her husband's name which had some cachet because the lord of the estate was Lord Grantham's cousin. While so employed, the mistress' lady's maid told Vera in error (major error!) about Mary's liaison with the Turkish Ambassador Kemal Pamuk.

At about the same time, Mr. Bates' mother died. Vera learned that the amount of Bates' inheritance was significant. Vera, ever the opportunist, unexpectedly visited Bates at Downton Abbey and threatened to disclose Lady Mary's shame unless Bates paid her significant sums for her silence. Vera also insisted that Bates return to London to live with her as she disliked living alone. Feeling trapped, and wanting to preserve the reputation of his employer, Bates chivalrously gave notice to Carson and left Downton Abbey to accompany his wife and save Mary's honor.

US LAW: *Extortion* is the crime of obtaining money or other property using threats to cause any of the following: physical injury, property damage; harm to a business, career or reputation; or exposure of a secret tending to subject a person to hate, contempt or ridicule. While the laws vary from state to state, extortion is typically viewed as akin to *larceny*, the more generic term for stealing money or property.

A related crime is coercion which consists of the same threats as for extortion but the wrongdoer's purpose is not obtaining money or property but rather, compelling a person to engage or refrain from engaging in certain conduct.

APPLICATION TO DA: Vera successfully extorted money from Mr. Bates in exchange for her silence on Mary's encounter with Pamuk. This constitutes the crime of extortion. However, to seek prosecution would have required exposure to at least the police of Mary's circumstances. Bates is too discreet with his master's secrets to pursue that course of action.

A problem with bargaining for nondisclosure of a secret is that Vera may reassert the disclosure threat repeatedly, seeking more money or property each time. Payment for silence is a deal with the devil.

In addition to money, Vera insisted on Bates' companionship. Extortion covers only property and money. One's company is intangible. In seeking Bates' time and attention, Vera was committing coercion.

Chapter 36

Forgery – Mr. Bates

DA FACTS: [5] The Prince of Wales regularly sent childish love letters to Lady Freda Dudley Ward, with whom he was having an affair. In a scene in which Julian Fellows mixed historical figures with fictional ones, Lady Freda discussed some of the letters with Rose. In her naiveté, and in the presence of Terence Samson, an acquaintance of Robert Crawley, Rose disclosed the existence of a compromising letter in the paramour's purse. While Lady Freda was dancing and Rose was meeting and greeting, Sampson surreptitiously removed the letter from the pocketbook. The note had the potential to greatly embarrass the Prince.

When Lady Freda informed Rose that the letter was missing, Rose suspected the cad Sampson. She spoke to Robert who no doubt correctly surmised that Sampson intended to profit from the note, either by blackmailing Mrs. Ward or selling the letter to foreign newspapers. Rose and Robert hatched a plan – he would occupy Sampson with a card game while Rose and Mary searched Sampson's flat for the communication. A potential stumbling block was gaining access to Sampson's apartment.

At the request of Robert, Bates drafted a note supposedly from Sampson to his landlord, authorizing the landlord to admit Rose and Mary to the house.

---
[5] This situation is also examined from a different legal perspective in Chapter 32.

The good news – the note did the trick and the two women gained entry. The bad news: they did not find the letter.

US LAW: Forgery is the crime of making, completing or altering a written document without authority and with the intent to deceive or injure another person. It includes creating a document such as a counterfeit dollar bill, altering a document such as changing the medication described in a doctor's prescription without the physician's authorization, or signing someone's name to a document without that person's permission.

APPLICATION TO DA: Unknown to Sampson, Bates created a document and signed Sampson's name to it. Bates objective was to deceive the landlord into believing Sampson had given permission for Mary and Rose to enter the flat. These acts constitute the crime of forgery.

Chapter 37

Impersonation – Major Patrick Gordon

A FACTS: A soldier with significant burns and injuries on his face came to Downton Abbey for recuperative services in 1918 when the estate served as a convalescent home for combatants. The soldier's face was partially wrapped in gauze which covered almost all of one side of his face, and a small part of the other side. The bandages hid much of the man's face making a positive visual identification impossible.

The name he gave when first admitted to the mansion was Major Patrick Gordon, a member of the Canadian Light Infantry. However, once inside the castle and having initiated conversation with Edith, he claimed to be Patrick Crawley who was engaged to Mary but reportedly died in the sinking of the Titanic.

Per Gordon's story, he survived the sinking but developed amnesia and, mistaken for a Canadian because of his accent, was sent to Downton Abbey. He claimed the amnesia developed after the ship sank and so he had lacked the mental recollection to dispute the Canadian connection. Per his narrative, he regained his memory after the war. He wooed Edith, telling her that Patrick loved her, not Mary, all along. Mary did not believe that he was Patrick Crawley.

Edith was less skeptical, wanting to believe him. Lord Grantham met the man and would have totally discredited his story except for an unusual gesture the man made that mimicked Patrick Crawley – wiping his lips with his fingers in a distinctive way.

Robert hired his attorney to investigate. The lawyer discovered that a Patrick Gordon once worked with the real Patrick Crawley at the Foreign Office, which explained how Gordon knew some of the private details and mannerisms of the unfortunate Titanic victim.

Major Patrick Gordon left Downton in a rush, without saying goodbye to Edith or any of his other hosts. Suspicion has it that burn victim Gordon sought to impersonate Patrick Crawley and thereby inherit Downton and all its riches.

US LAW: Posing as someone other than oneself for the purpose of securing a benefit or injuring someone else is a crime in most states. Often called *criminal impersonation*, the crime typically consists of pretending to be another person with intent to obtain a benefit, or injure or defraud another.

APPLICATION TO DA: Major Patrick Gordon presumably was not Patrick Crawley. Had he been successful in convincing the Crawleys that he was the rightful heir of Downton Abbey, he would have benefited significantly from his deception, which was his intention. Gordon's attempt to assume the identity of the would-be inheritor of the estate constituted criminal impersonation.

Chapter 38

Larceny – Thomas

DA FACTS: Isis was the name of Robert's trusty dog, a handsome yellow lab. Thomas, out of favor with Robert, hid Isis in a shack, intending to find and return the dog after Lord Grantham realized Isis' absence. Thomas hoped thereby to regain Robert's good graces and possibly win a promotion to valet. The plan backfired when a village girl found Isis and brought the pooch to the Earl. To the frustration of Thomas' detractors, Robert nonetheless credited Thomas with searching for the dog and rehired him.

US LAW: This vignette illustrates well the necessary two elements of a crime. Every crime consists of a wrongful act and a *criminal mental state*, usually meaning that the defendant acted intentionally. No defendant can be convicted unless the jury, or judge in a bench trial, is convinced beyond a reasonable doubt that both elements are present.

The wrongful act for the crime of *larceny* is taking someone else's property without permission. The criminal mental state is intent to deprive the owner of property and appropriate the stolen property for the thief's use.

APPLICATION TO DA: The facts of this scenario do not constitute larceny. While Thomas committed the wrongful act of taking Lord Grantham's canine, Thomas did not intend to deprive the Earl of the dog indefinitely nor to appropriate Isis to his own use. Instead, Thomas intended to return the dog to Robert so Thomas could appear to be a hero of sorts and endear himself again to Robert.

Chapter 39

Murder and Manslaughter – Titanic Crew

A FACTS: As the Titanic was weakening from flooding prior to sinking, some crew members locked and guarded barriers that segregated accommodations for third class passengers from those of first and second class. The former were mostly poor immigrants coming to America seeking a better life, while the latter were middle class or wealthy. The result was hundreds of passengers were trapped and unable to exit their quarters while the ship sank. The disturbing explanation for this action was to prevent the lower-paying passengers from rushing the lifeboats.

US LAW: The crews' actions arguably would constitute *manslaughter or depraved indifference murder*. Manslaughter consists of recklessly causing someone's death. *Reckless* means to appreciate and disregard a substantial risk of death. Depraved indifference murder applies where a person not only recklessly causes death but does so by engaging in conduct that creates a grave risk of death in a manner evidencing a depraved indifference to human life. In effect, it requires a greater degree of recklessness.

Unlike civil liability, criminal responsibility does not survive a person's death.

APPLICATION TO DA: By blocking the partitions, the crew was likely meting out a death sentence to the trapped passengers. They were deprived of the possibility of getting up to the main deck and boarding a life boat. They faced certain drowning when the waters flooding the ship from below reached their deck. A good argument could be made that such action constituted depraved indifference murder. At the least, the behavior constitutes manslaughter. However, few of the crew survived so those blocking the door likely did not live to face criminal prosecution.

Chapter 40

Promoting Prison Contraband – Durant and Craig

FACTS: Durant was the crooked prison guard who policed John Bates while imprisoned for supposedly killing his first wife Vera. Durant was a drug dealer who collaborates with Bates' cellmate Craig. Working together, they brought illegal drugs into the prison and sold it to prisoners.

US LAW: Illegal drugs in prison remain a problem today in the United States. Inventive inmates, complicit visitors and corrupt staff perpetuate this phenomenon. A crime exists called promoting prison contraband. It applies to both prisoners and nonprisoners. For prisoners, the crime consists of knowingly and unlawfully making, obtaining or possessing any item that is illegal to possess or transport in jail. For nonprisoners, the crime is committed by knowingly and unlawfully introducing contraband into a detention facility.

APPLICATION TO DA: Both Durant and Bates' roommate are guilty of promoting prison contraband.

Chapter 41

Social Gambling – Terence Sampson and Michael Gregson

A FACTS: Terence Sampson was an acquaintance of Robert Crawley from his gentlemen's club in London. Although Robert did not think highly of Terrence, the latter was invited to a house party at Downton Abbey. While there, Sampson played poker with Lord Grantham, Lord Gillingham and John Bullock. Sampson swindled the trio out of substantial amounts money and left the table with their IOUs. Robert was stung by the extent of his loss and planned to hide it from Cora. Edith's married beau, Michael Gregson, comes to the rescue. He insisted on another round of cards and out-swindled Sampson, winning back the IOUs of the others plus additional money from Sampson. Gregson canceled the promissory notes and took one from Sampson. The next morning, at the insistence of Edith, Gregson canceled Sampson's note as well. The details of the stings were not revealed.

US LAW: While many types of gambling are outlawed in most states, social gambling is distinguished from casino gambling. With social gambling, there is no promoter who is paid for hosting the game. Instead, social gambling involves wagering among buddies, typically a friendly poker game, and all the money gambled is paid to winners.

Approximately 20 states outlaw social gambling; the other 30 permit it. Some states limit the amount of permissible bets in social gambling, and some limit the maximum amount a player may win or lose in a 24 hour period (e.g. Iowa has a $50 cap).

Many states prohibit even social gambling in bars, primarily to limit bad betting decisions fueled by alcohol. Some states permit social gambling in bars provided the bar has a social gambling license. The bars are prohibited from charging an entrance fee when social gambling is allowed, and cannot be compensated for hosting the play.

APPLICATION TO DA: The poker game at Downton Abbey appears to be a classic example of social gambling. The game was played among friends and acquaintances. All the money wagered was paid to the winner; the house did not take or receive a share for sponsoring the event. Such gambling in a majority of the states is legal, but is illegal in 20. Given the usual private, in-home locale of such games, prosecution of violations is very limited.

Chapter 42

Sodomy and Related Sex Crimes – Thomas

FACTS: Thomas Barrow, the Under Footman, is homosexual, which was not common or socially accepted at the time that the Downton Abbey series was situated. He had a fling with Phillip, Duke of Crowborough. In another sexual encounter, Thomas was led to believe by Mrs. O'Brien that James was likewise gay and interested in a rendezvous with Thomas. He snuck into James' room and kissed him on the lips while James was asleep. Alfred, another employee, walked in at that very moment. James awoke, quickly realized what was happening, and angrily banished Thomas. Alfred reported his observations to Carson, who stated he consideed Thomas "something foul." Thomas was almost fired over the incident.

US LAW: Most states had a crime called *consensual sodomy*, meaning oral and anal sex engaged in willingly by each partner. Most states have repealed these laws, recognizing that consenting adults should be free to make their own decisions. In 2003 the United States Supreme Court decided the case of *Lawrence v. Texas* which recognized personal autonomy by declaring void a Texas statute that criminalized consensual intimate sexual conduct. The decision was grounded on the constitutional right of privacy and liberty. Forcible (nonconsensual) sodomy remains illegal in every state. (So too is forcible sexual conduct between a male and a female). Also illegal is unwanted touching of any *intimate body part* for the purpose of sexual gratification. "Intimate body parts" are typically described as genital or anal areas, groin, inner thigh, or buttock of any person, or the breast of a female.

APPLICATION TO DA: The weekend dalliance between Thomas and Phillip was consensual and therefore not criminal or otherwise illegal in the United States today. The kiss on James' lips, while nonconsensual, apparently did not involve an intimate body part. Therefore, with few exceptions, the kiss would likely not constitute a sexual crime. The act would constitute the civil wrong of battery which means unwanted touching of any body part.

Chapter 43

Speeding – Mathew

FACTS: After Mathew finished cooing with Mary in the hospital over the beauty of their newborn son, Mathew was very excited to tell the family. While racing back from the hospital to Downton Abbey, he encountered another car on the road, lost control of his vehicle, and rolled down a hill. Very sadly, he was killed in the accident.

US LAW: Every state and locality sets speed limits on roads, and dedicates some portion of law enforcement resources to enforcement of those laws. Motorists who drive in excess of the specified speed risk being ticketed for the violation. Penalties typically include a fine, *surcharge* (a fee for the "privilege" of using the courts), and points on the driver's license. If motorists accumulate a specified number of points within a designated time period, their driving license may be suspended or revoked. For example, if a New York driver accrues 11 points in 18 months, the license will be suspended.

The number of points associated with a speeding ticket is dependent on how many miles above the speed limit the driver was traveling. The greater the speed, the more points will be assessed. Also in many states, if the motorist accumulates a certain number of speeding convictions within a designated time period, the license will be suspended. For example, in New York three speeding convictions in 18 months will result in suspension.

Speed limits vary depending on the type of roadway. Factors reviewed when speed limits are set include the number of lanes on the road, whether the roadway is a two way highway, the number of curb cuts in the area, the number of vehicles that typically use the road, and whether the area is residential, commercial, or undeveloped.

The purpose of speeding laws is to keep everyone safe on the roadways by reducing the possibility of accidents. When a driver is proceeding too fast for conditions, the chances of an accident increase.

APPLICATION TO DA: The scene involving Mathew's death underscores the concerns about speeding. Had he not been exceeding the speed limit, he may have been able to retain control of his vehicle and avoid the deadly accident. He paid dearly for his excessive pace.

Chapter 44

Spitting – Train Station

DA FACTS: At the train station near Downton Abbey, a sign was prominently displayed on the railroad platform that read, "Spitting Is Illegal." Every time one of the characters took the train out of town, the sign was clearly visible.

US LAW: Many states and municipalities have passed legislation that outlaws spitting. Most of the statutes were enacted more than 100 years ago to fight the spread of various diseases. Sputum can spread infectious diseases such as tuberculosis, pneumonia, and bronchitis. The risk to people in current times is considered by most authorities very small. One possibility – someone steps in spit, puts their shoes on a bus seat, and another passenger puts his hand on the seat. It is easy to overstate the risks.

Massachusetts passed an anti-spit statute in 1886 as part of the commonwealth's crimes against public health, and the law still remains in effect. The penalty is a fine of not more than $20. New York City has a similar ordinance. Violation can result in a $25 fine and a maximum of ten days in jail. The amount of these fines is small by today's standards but were significant in earlier times when the laws were first adopted. Minneapolis City Council repealed its anti-spitting law in June, 2015. Chicago did the same in 1997.

Not many law enforcement resources are directed towards enforcing these laws. Police have other more serious issues to address. Said one municipal government official, "Enforcement depends on the officer's discretion. We don't drive down the street looking for people spitting." Nonetheless, occasional prosecutions do occur, and sometimes the statutes are used in *plea bargaining*, that is, a defendant charged with a more serious offense is provided the opportunity to plead to the reduced charge of spitting as a way to resolve the matter without trial. Such plea bargains are offered to save time and money by resolving the case without a trial. Typically, such offers are made to a defendant with either no criminal record or a very limited record, or in a situation where the prosecutor has proof problems on the higher charge.

With the advent of HIV, new laws addressed towards spitting were adopted in 11 states. They prohibit spitting, biting or throwing bodily fluids including saliva by people with HIV. Those states are Georgia, Indiana, Louisiana, Missouri, Mississippi, Nebraska, Ohio, Pennsylvania, South Carolina, South Dakota, and Utah.

APPLICATION TO DA: If anyone spits in a train station in a locality where it is outlawed, the chances of prosecution are limited. If a charge is pursued, the penalty would likely be a small fine. If the person spitting has HIV and the violations occurs in one of the 11 listed states, the seriousness of the crime will be significantly elevated.

Chapter 45

Tampering with a Witness – Audrey Bartlett

A FACTS: Audrey Bartlett was one of Vera Bates' few friends. They lived in the same neighborhood. Vera died from ingesting rat poison that was cooked in a pie. Mr. Bates had bought the poison and was convicted of killing Vera. His claim that Vera committed suicide was rejected by the court. Bartlett however had critical evidence that would exonerate Mr. Bates. Bartlett had seen Vera making the crust of the fatal dessert in the evening of Mr. Bates' visit after he had left by train for Downton Abbey. This established that Vera poisoned herself and Mr. Bates was innocent.

The information became known to the prison guard and Bates' cell mate. They had issues with Mr. Bates and so, appallingly, convinced Bartlett not to disclose to Mr. Bates' attorney what she had seen.

Mr. Bates figured out what the guard and his roommate had done. Bates threatened to report their actions to prison officials which would likely trigger both an extension of the cellmate's prison term and firing of the guard. They were convinced to encourage Bartlett to tell the authorities what she saw. Her evidence was sufficient to exonerate Bates.

US LAW: Most states have adopted a crime of tampering with a witness. The crime consists of threatening or assaulting a witness to encourage her not to attend court and thereby avoid testifying. The crime also includes encouraging by force a witness to swear falsely. The crime can be a misdemeanor or felony depending in part on the degree of force used to convince the witness to either avoid testifying or *perjure* herself (testify falsely under oath).

APPLICATION TO DA: The cellmate and guard likely committed the crime of tampering with a witness. Assuming they threatened or otherwise used force to discourage Bartlett from disclosing to the authorities the exculpatory information, the cellmate and the guard would be guilty.

Chapter 46

Tampering with Evidence – Mary

A FACTS: Anna gave to Mrs. Hughes for donation to charity a coat worn by Mr. Bates. Mrs. Hughes checked the pockets and discovered a train ticket from York to London for the day Green died. This appeared to place Bates at the scene of Green's murder, and if so, would be damning evidence. Mrs. Hughes informed Mary and gave her the ticket. Mary felt compelled to disclose to the authorities the existence of the ticket until Bates played an instrumental and indispensable role in retrieving a love letter sent by the Prince of Wales to Freda Dudley Ward, the Prince's mistress. The letter had been finagled away from Rose by the manipulative Terence Sampson. Mary, believing she was eliminating incriminating evidence against Bates, showed her family's gratitude by throwing the ticket into a fire in her bedroom fireplace.

US LAW: Tampering With Evidence Is A Crime. The Outlawed Conduct Is Knowingly Destroying A Document Or Record With The Intent Of Interfering With A Possible Investigation Or One That Is Already In Progress. To Convict, A Prosecutor Must Prove That The Defendant Intended To Disrupt An Investigation. The Crime Also Includes Making False Entries In Records, And Modifying Documents To Hide Illegal Activity Or Avoid Payments, Or Deleting Emails. In Many States, The Crime Is A Felony. A Person Who Tampers With Evidence In A Federal Case Faces Up To 20 Years In Prison. Penalties In State

Courts Are Typically Less Harsh But Nonetheless Substantial. A Defense To The Crime Is That Defendant Lacked Knowledge That The Destroyed Or Damaged Evidence Was, In Fact, Evidence Of Criminal Activity.

APPLICATION TO DA: Mary Was Aware Of The Investigation Surrounding Green's Death And The Potential Significance Of The Ticket. Her Intention In Destroying It Was To Protect Bates From Prosecution. Had The Ticket Been Incriminating To Mr. Bates (Which In Fact It Was Not), Mary Would Be Guilty Of Tampering With Evidence.

Chapter 47

Terrorism – Branson

A FACTS: Tom Branson had strong political leanings. He confided to Sybil that he wanted to bridge the income gap between the aristocracy and the poor. He identified Robert as part of the evil "oppressive class" but, to assuage Sybil, added that Robert was "a good man and a decent employer." Tom was an Irish sympathizer, believing that Ireland should exist as a country independent from England. As such, he attended republican meetings in Ireland where violent protests were advocated for the purpose of intimidating and coercing England to release Ireland from its control. Additionally, Tom was present when Irish Republican protestors set fire to an aristocratic family's house. As a result of these actions, Tom was wanted by the Irish police. He was able to avoid arrest by escaping to Downton Abbey.

US LAW: Terrorism is defined as the unlawful use of force or violence against persons or property to intimidate or coerce a government, the civilian population, or any segment thereof, done to advance political or social objectives. The purpose of terrorism is to intimidate a population and thereby compel a government or an international organization to do or abstain from doing some desired act. Terrorism exploits human fear to help achieve the terrorists' goals.

APPLICATION TO DA: Acts of arson qualify as terrorism when done to intimidate the populace and coerce a government such as England to take some action desired by the terrorists, such as granting Ireland its independence. Had Tom set the fire, he would be guilty. If he was merely a bystander sympathetic to the cause but did not offer assistance or otherwise aid the actors, he would not be liable.

Criminal Law Procedure

Chapter 48

Alibi – Mr. Bates

DA FACTS: Mr. Bates was a suspect in the killing of Mr. Green, given Bates' anger about Green sexually assaulting Anna. When Anna was imprisoned, Bates falsely confessed to the murder to win her freedom. However, Mosley and Baxter visited sixty plus pubs and eventually found a server who recognized Bates' picture and remembered his limp. The waiter's recollection established that Bates was eating lunch at a pub in York at the time of the killing in London, and so could not possibly have committed the murder.

US LAW: An alibi is a defense to a legal action consisting of proof that the accused was somewhere other than the scene of the crime at the time the crime was committed. If the alibi is proven, the defendant could not have committed the crime.

Most states' laws require notice to the prosecutor when a defendant intends to prevent evidence of an alibi at trial. This gives the prosecutor time to investigate the alibi and prepare to refute it, if possible. Typically, the notice is required to identify the place where defendant claims to have been at the time of the crime, and the name and contact information of every witness who has knowledge about the alibi. If the prosecution's investigation generates any witnesses who can rebut defendant's alibi, the prosecutor must so inform the defendant, including witnesses' names and contact information.

APPLICATION TO DA: The testimony of the pub waiter, stating that Mr. Bates was eating lunch in York at the time of Green's death, constitutes an alibi. If Bates was charged with the murder, his attorney would need to give notice to the prosecutor of the intention to present proof of an alibi at trial. In response, the prosecutor would need to disclose to the defense names and contact information of any witnesses who can rebut the alibi witnesses. Each side can then investigate the alibi evidence prior to trial so each can be prepared.

Chapter 49

Circumstantial Evidence – John Pegg and Vera Bates

DA FACTS: Isobel imposed on Violet to hire John Pegg as a gardener's assistant. Two items went missing - first a letter opener and then a small ivory figurine. Violet was convinced that Pegg was the thief and fired him. The figurine was then discovered in the maid's cleaning bucket where it had fallen. Isobel was upset for Pegg and was perennially peeved by Violet. Isobel went hunting for the letter opener. She finagled her way into Violet's house and searched for the missing item. Sure enough, she found it under a couch cushion. The story ended happily. The Dowager apologized and rehired Pegg.

ADDITIONAL DA FACTS: Following derailed divorce proceedings between Mr. Bates and Vera, Mr. Bates went to London to confront her. He returns to Downton sporting a large scratch on his face. He tells Anna the meeting went terribly. The next day Vera is discovered dead from ingested rat poisoning. Bates had purchased the poison the day before. The police are convinced that Bates murdered his wife and charge him with the homicide. He is convicted and sentenced to death, but the sentence is commuted to one of life in prison. Eventually his innocence is established and he is released from jail.

Karen Morris Esq. & Sandra Williams Esq.

US LAW: *Circumstantial evidence* refers to a series of facts and circumstances from which another fact can be deduced or reasonably inferred. Contrast circumstantial evidence with *direct evidence,* which refers to testimony of an eyewitness or a participant that, if believed, proves a fact directly without the need to draw any inferences.

Assume a murder has occurred. If a witness observed the perpetrator pull the trigger of a gun and cause the death of a person, that would constitute direct evidence. If however a witness sees two people go into an empty room, the door is closed, a shot rings out, and one of the two is dead on the floor, this is circumstantial evidence that the survivor committed the murder.

The law provides that both direct and circumstantial evidence are acceptable as a means of proving a fact. The jury, or judge in a *bench trial* (a case with no jury), must decide whether or not to draw the suggested inference. The inference from circumstantial evidence does not always prove true.

APPLICATION TO DA: The fact that Violet was missing two items from her home close in time to hiring a new gardener's assistant suggests that the assistant took the missing items. Violet was quick to draw that inference. Fortunately for Pegg, Isobel donned her sleuth cap and saved the day.

Similarly, circumstantial evidence suggested that Mr. Bates killed Vera. The police, jury and judge drew the inference from the available facts that he caused her death. As we know, he spent time in jail wrongfully because the inference was not accurate.

Chapter 50

Exoneration: Post Conviction Relief – Mr. Bates

A FACTS: Audrey Bartlett was one of Vera Bates' few friends. Audrey lived around the corner from Vera. Audrey had critical evidence that would exonerate Mr. Bates from Vera's murder. Vera died from ingesting rat poison. Mr. Bates was convicted of killing her by allegedly using the rat poison, which he had admittedly bought. He however claimed his wife committed suicide. Anna discovered that Bartlett had seen Vera making the crust of the fatal pie in the evening, after Mr. Bates had left by train for Downton. This established that Vera poisoned herself and would clear Mr. Bates.

The information became known to the prison guard and bates' cell mate. They had their own issues with mr. Bates and so, appallingly, convinced bartlett not to disclose to mr. Bates' attorney what she had seen.

Mr. Bates figured out what the guard and his roommate had done. Bates threatened to report their actions to prison officials which would result in extension of the cellmate's prison term and firing of the guard. They were thus convinced to change their attitude and encourage bartlett to tell the authorities what she saw. Her evidence was sufficient to exonerate mr. Bates.

US LAW: exoneration, also called post conviction relief, means a person convicted of a crime is later proved to be innocent. One reason this happens is newly discovered evidence. The evidence must be of such a type that it could not have been discovered and produced by defendant at trial even with the exercise of due diligence. Further, it must be such as to create a probability that, had the evidence been available at trial, the verdict would have been in defendant's favor. The judge typically orders a hearing to determine if the new evidence satisfies these requirements.

APPLICATION TO DA: at the time of the trial, bartlett had not disclosed that she saw vera making the deadly pie, and bates had no way of knowing what bartlett saw. That evidence was not revealed until after the trial and conviction. It was of such a nature that it probably would have resulted in a verdict in bates' favor. Thus, as occurred, bates was rightfully exonerated.

Chapter 51

Death Penalty – Mr. Bates

DA FACTS: Mr. Bates was convicted (wrongly) of murder for poisoning his estranged wife, Vera. He was sentenced to be hanged but was granted a reprieve of life in prison. The death penalty at the time was mandatory in England.

US LAW: Currently in the United States, 31 states authorize the death penalty, and 19 do not. The United States Supreme Court has ruled that the death penalty is not a per se violation of the right against cruel and unusual punishment contained in the Eight Amendment to the United States Constitution. Instead, execution fulfills the social purposes of retribution and deterrence, although the latter is subject to debate.

To pass muster, a penalty must be proportional to the crime. In accessing the suitability of a particular penalty, courts evaluate the offense's gravity, the penalty's strictness, and how the state punishes other crimes. To fulfill the proportionality requirement, death penalty is used almost exclusively for murder.

Most states do not impose the death penalty unless one or more aggravating factors exist in a murder case. Aggravating factors vary somewhat from state to state but typically include killing more than one person; killing a police officer; killing a witness; killing a head of state or other senior public official; torturing the victim prior to the murder; previous conviction of a violent felony involving a firearm; previous conviction of two serious offenses; and vulnerable victim due to age, youth or infirmity.

Various methods of execution exist, including the electric chair, lethal injection, hanging, firing squad, and gas chamber. Typically, the state legislature determines the method to be used. The manner must not inflict unnecessary pain.

A problem with the death penalty is its disproportionate application on racial grounds, or stated differently, unequal justice. For example, In 2014 there were 35 executions in the United States Of those, 43% were black or Hispanic, who make up only 30% of the country's population. A California study found that defendants who killed whites were over three times more likely to be sentenced to death than those who killed blacks, and over four times more likely than those who killed Latinos. Some states have declared a moratorium on executions until further study is completed on discriminatory application and ways to stop it. In those states, the substitute penalty is life in prison without the possibility of parole.

APPLICATION TO DA: Had Bates killed his wife, the murder would not have qualified for the death penalty in the United States because it lacked an aggravating factor.

Chapter 52

False Confessions – Mr. Bates

DA FACTS: When Anna was imprisoned as a suspect in the killing of Green, Bates could not bear to see his wife in jail. To win her release, he confessed, falsely, to the murder. Anna was then released from jail.

US LAW: A *false confession* is an admission of guilt for a crime the confessor did not commit. Perhaps surprisingly, the number of false confessions among criminal defendants is significant. A variety of factors cause people to admit to a crime they did not commit. These include duress, coercion by the police, fear of violence or actual infliction of harm by the police, the threat of a harsh sentence, diminished capacity due to alcohol or drugs, mental impairment, or misunderstanding of the situation.

Police have a duty to investigate fully the circumstances of a crime, and cannot accept a confession as accurate without confirmation. The law in most states precludes a conviction based exclusively on a confession. Instead, additional evidence is required that the crime was in fact committed.

APPLICATION TO DA: Bates' confession was not the result of coercion or threats on the part of the police. Instead, it was knowingly and voluntarily made, albeit with a specific objective in mind. Evidence of the crime clearly exists – Green's death under suspicious circumstances. Fortunately, Mosley and Baxter found proof that Bates was eating at a pub in York at the time of Green's death, and so could not possibly have committed a murder in London.

Chapter 53

Handwriting Experts – Terence Sampson

A FACTS:[6] The devious Terence Sampson (the card shark who was upstaged by Atticus) swiped a romantic letter Rose had in her pocketbook written by the Prince of Wales and addressed to his paramour, Freda Dudley Ward. Rose advised Robert that the letter was missing. He immediately perceived the potential public relations disaster for the British monarchy if the letter was leaked to the press. To save the crown, Robert and Mary developed a plan to search Sampson's apartment for the dispatch. To get past the doorman, Robert solicited Bates' assistance in *forging* (creating a writing without authority) a letter supposedly from Sampson authorizing Mary to enter the living quarters. Bates was up to the task. The doorman was fooled, and Mary gained entry.

US LAW: A handwriting expert is someone who is trained to compare a questioned document or signature against a known document or signature. An expert witness may be called to the witness stand by a party to a lawsuit only when the subject matter relates to a science, profession, occupation or business that is not within the knowledge or understanding of the average person. Handwriting analysis qualifies.

---

6 This situation is also examined from a different legal perspective in Chapter 32 and 36.

Handwriting analysts can help determine who wrote a document or, in some cases, who did not write it. They also analyze documents for signs of alteration or forgery. The witnesses are used in cases where the author of a document is unknown or when documents are suspected of being forged. Examples of the types of cases they can be helpful with are unauthorized check cashing, questionable signatures on a will, contracts or other documents that appear to have been modified, or any time the legitimacy of a signature is questioned. Handwriting analysts might also be consulted to determine if graffiti or a threatening note was the work of a particular suspect.

The fundamental foundation of handwriting analysis is that every person has a unique writing style. The witness's opinion relies on significant knowledge of the way people form letters, which characteristics of letter formation are unique, and the ways in which a person's fine-motor skills can affect his handwriting and thus leave clues about an author's identity.

Handwriting experts can seek certification through the Association of Certified Fraud Examiners, and the Scientific Association of Forensic Examiners, among other accrediting bodies.

As with any expert witness, a handwriting expert must be *qualified* (proven to have sufficient credentials and expertise) before he can testify to an opinion in court. To qualify, the expert must have specialized knowledge, skill, experience, training and/or education sufficient to qualify as an expert on the subject This requires testimony about the proposed expert's educational and professional background and experience. Minimally, the expert witness must be familiar with underlying methodology and procedures employed and relied upon in the field, and refer to them as a basis for the opinion. In other words, the witness' opinion must be based upon a reasonable degree of scientific certainty.

Nothing in the proposed expert's background is exempt from scrutiny. An expert may be prevented from testifying when unable to show a reliable basis for his theory of the case, or where there are grounds to doubt his competence.

APPLICATION TO DA: If Sampson sued Mary for trespass and sought to establish that the signature on the note to the landlord was a fraud, Sampson would need a qualified expert handwriting witness.

Chapter 54

Police Line-Ups – Anna

A FACTS: Investigator Vyner was actively investigating Mr. Green's death. Anna was asked to stop by at Scotland Yard while in London attending the wedding of Rose and Atticus. She concurred and was hoodwinked into participating in a line-up, called in England an ID parade. Surprisingly, a supposed eye witness identified Anna as the person who pushed Green to his death.

US LAW: A *line-up* is an investigative technique used by police to help identify a perpetrator. A witness or victim observes a group, typically 5-6 individuals with similar characteristics. Witnesses are then asked whether anyone in the identity parade is the accused.

A line-up can be live where the people to be observed line up against a wall. A more common method of handling line-ups is to conduct a photo array, meaning the police present the witness a set of photographs of people who have physical traits akin to those of the suspect. The witness then identifies which if any picture portrays the alleged wrongdoer.

The *due process clause* of the federal Constitution requires fair court proceedings. It encompasses certain rights of the suspect when in a line-up. They include the following. The line-up must not be unduly suggestive of the suspect's identity. Instead, the people or photos in the lineup should appear similar to the suspect, meaning the people should be of similar age, and have similar skin coloration, hair color, height, weight, and other like distinguishing characteristics. A suspect has the right to the presence of an attorney. The lawyer can help ensure that the suspect's rights are not violated. The officer who conducts the line-up should not be the official in charge of the investigation. This rule helps to prevent an over-zealous officer from compromising the defendant's rights in an effort to obtain a positive identification from a witness.

If the suspect's rights are violated during the line-up, the remedy is *suppression*, meaning the identification cannot be used by the prosecution as evidence at trial. If the prosecutor does not have another means to identify the suspect as the wrongdoer, the case against the suspect will be dismissed.

A suspect is not required to participate in a line-up and can decline to do so. Likewise, a person who is not a suspect can refuse take part. A *defendant* (a suspect who was arrested prior to the line-up) can be required to participate.

APPLICATION TO DA: Anna, who was a police suspect but not a defendant, could have declined to participate in the ID parade. Her circumstances demonstrate the risks of agreeing to do so. Had she requested an attorney, she no doubt would have been advised to decline participation.

Chapter 55

Prison Mail – Mr. Bates

A FACTS: While Bates was in jail for the supposed murder of his first wife Vera, he was distraught because he had received no letters from Anna. This despite the fact he had sent her many, and, unbeknownst to him, she had written him every day. Both were bewildered. Bates believed Anna's love for him was waning, and Anna believed Bates was being gallant and wanting her to go on with her life without him.

Turns out Bates' cell mate has partnered with one of the guards in a drug dealing ring inside the prison. In revenge for thwarting a plot to pin a drug possession on Bates, the cellmate convinced the guard that Bates should be on a watch list of dangerous criminals. Apparently prisoners on that list are denied mail or visitors.

US LAW: The right of free speech in the First Amendment of the United States Constitution entitles prisoners to receive and send mail. However, prison officials may place reasonable restrictions on these rights. Permissible limitations allow jail personnel to inspect the mail to maintain prison security and check for contraband. A jail can censor letters or withhold delivery when necessary to protect the facility's security, and if the censorship process includes appropriate procedural safeguards. So, to maintain prison security and check for contraband, prison officials may open inmate's incoming mail provided an institutional policy exists for doing so and the policy is applied evenly to all inmates. For the same security reasons, prisons can limit the type and amount of mail a prisoner is able to receive. Always, a legitimate reason must exist for interfering with a prisoner's incoming mail. Arbitrary interference based on a guard's personal biases, and reading mail merely to harass a prisoner violate the prisoner's free speech rights.

Concerning outgoing mail, restrictions must meet a more exacting standard than limitations on incoming mail. They must be no greater than necessary or essential to protect an important or substantial government interest.

Restrictions on *privileged mail* are more limited than non-privileged mail. Privileged mail includes communications with the prisoner's attorney and is entitled to greater confidentiality and freedom from censorship.

APPLICATION TO DA: While Bates' prison could review his mail and redact it if necessary for legitimate public safety reasons, there is no justification for withholding all incoming and outgoing mail. Harassment of an inmate by an irritated guard is not legal grounds to interfere with the flow of mail. The action of the guards in refusing to deliver Bates' mail violates prisoners' rights.

Miscellaneous

Chapter 56

Conscientious Objector – Branson

A FACTS: Branson was summoned by the war office in England. Being Irish, he did not want to fight for the British Army and planned on becoming a conscientious objector. Instead, Branson was rejected by the military due to a heart murmur, a physical condition linked to heart valve issues.

US LAW: The United States Constitution gives the federal government the power to raise an army, and also to draft people to fight in wars. In 1973, Congress abolished the draft in favor of an all voluntary force. As a result, only those who want to enlist in the armed forces enter the military. Thus, no one currently needs to pursue an exemption from service by seeking conscientious objector status.

When the military draft is in effect, a person seeking to qualify as a conscientious objector must demonstrate a "firm, fixed and sincere objection" to participation in either war in any form, or the bearing of arms. The source of the objection must be a moral, ethical, or religious belief or training. Political, sociological and philosophical views do not qualify. Thinking that war is illogical or a bad policy is not sufficient.

War must conflict with the objector's personal values. The opposition must be to all wars. One who objects only to a particular war or wars does not qualify as a conscientious objector under US law.

Karen Morris Esq. & Sandra Williams Esq.

The process to obtain conscientious objector status includes submission of an application and supporting documentation, interviews with a psychiatrist or other mental health specialist, a military chaplain, and an investigating officer, followed by a hearing. If any negative recommendations issue, the applicant has an opportunity to submit a rebuttal. Ultimately a decision is made by a Conscientious Objector Review Board.

Among the questions a would-be objector will be asked include the following: What do you believe about participation in war? How did your beliefs develop (what events, factors influenced you to believe this)? How does your life reflect those beliefs (How do your beliefs influence decisions or choices you make daily)?

If conscientious objector status is granted, service to the country is still required, called alternative service or noncombatant service. The non-fighter will either serve in the Army without using weapons or handling ammunition, such as in the medical corps, or will do "civilian work contributing to the maintenance of the national health, safety or interest."[7]

APPLICATION TO DA: Branson's objection to fighting for England would not have qualified for conscientious objector status. He was not opposed to all wars, but rather to fighting for a country whose policies he did not endorse. His objections were based on politics and his own personal philosophy about England. As a result, Branson was lucky he had a medical basis for avoiding service.

---

7 Military Selective Service Act.

Chapter 57

Conversion Therapy – Thomas

DA FACTS: Under-butler Thomas Barrows responded to a newspaper advertisement for a product called Choosing Your Own Path that claimed to reverse homosexuality. He ingested the supposed medication, and it caused him severe pain. The touted cure proved to be bogus and ineffective.

US LAW: Over the years many charlatans, and also some well-meaning people, have attempted to "cure" people of homosexuality. Current science recognizes that being gay is not a mental disease that can be cured or eliminated. Further, the American Psychological Association warns that efforts to change sexual orientation through therapy have "serious potential to harm young people because they present the view that the sexual orientation of lesbian, gay and bisexual youth is a mental illness or disorder."

A once-popular method of alleged treatment was called conversion therapy, also known as reparative therapy. The term refers to a range of treatments intended to transform sexual orientation from homosexual to heterosexual. Conversion therapy is not taught in accredited psychiatric or mental health training programs, and leading medical groups have denounced it. Some states have outlawed the treatments by statute including Oregon (which has the country's first openly bisexual governor), California, Illinois, New Jersey, Vermont and Washington DC. New York's governor used his *executive authority* (power inherent in being elected as a governor) to bar health care insurers from covering the practice, and prohibit mental health facilities from utilizing it on minors. Some local governments have also passed bans including Miami Beach, Florida.

APPLICATION TO DA: If Thomas lived in a state that prohibits conversion therapy, he could have saved his money and avoided the physical pain and false hope represented by the treatments he undertook. Also, if he lived now, happily he would have enjoyed a much greater degree of acceptance and presumably avoided his apparent self-loathing.

Chapter 58

Deed of Transference – Cora

FACTS: When Robert and Cora married, a significant part of the original attraction for Robert was Cora's money. Downton Abbey was in need of a monetary infusion and Cora was a wealthy woman. When Patrick and James Crawley succumbed with the Titanic, the entail dictated that Downton Abbey would be inherited by an unknown relative. The future of Cora and her daughters following Robert's eventual death thus became very uncertain. The women would have been much less concerned if they could count on access to Cora's money. But that was not possible. The funds had been given to Robert by a *Deed of Transference* which means that Cora's money became irrevocably tied to the land and buildings, and could not be removed.

US LAW: When a person makes a gift, ownership of the gifted item transfers from the donor to the recipient. That transfer gives the donee the right to control the property to the exclusion of the donor. In England this was called a Deed of Transference.

In the US, the term "deed" is used primarily to reference the transfer of real property, meaning land and buildings. We do not use deeds to transfer money or personal property. But the completion of a gift vests in the beneficiary all rights of ownership to the exclusion of the benefactor.

Karen Morris Esq. & Sandra Williams Esq.

APPLICATION TO DA: Robert, as the beneficiary of Cora's monetary gift, controlled the money once it was received. It was vested in Downton Abbey, the family home. The gift of money from Cora could not thereafter be revoked or separated.

Chapter 59

Eviction – Timothy Drewe

FACTS: The Drewe family had rented land at Downton Abbey for a long time, but the payments were in serious arrears. When the senior Mr. Drewe died, Mary and Tom decided to *foreclose on the lease*, meaning retake possession of the land and remove the Drewes as tenants. At the funeral, Mr. Drewe's surviving son told Robert that he would like to assume the tenancy and farm the land. Robert responded that the decision to terminate the lease had already been made. The young Drewe insisted he had not been aware of his father's debts and implored Robert to reconsider. Lord Grantham reluctantly agreed. Drewe tried but was unable to bring the account fully current. He convinced Lord Grantham to lend him the balance.

US LAW: Due dates for rent payments are typically made clear at the time a landlord-tenant relationship is begun. Significant or frequent delays in paying rent is grounds for *eviction*, meaning termination of the lease and removal of the tenant from the premises. Other grounds for eviction include causing damage to the property, frequently making loud noise or otherwise disturbing neighbors and other tenants, using the property for illegal purposes such as drug sales or prostitution, and violating the lease in some other significant way.

When landlords have grounds to evict, they cannot just oust the tenant from the premises. Instead, a landlord must first get a court order of eviction.

This requires the landlord to present to a judge proof of the grounds for eviction, and entitles the tenant to present any defense he might have.

If the landlord proves entitlement to the eviction, the tenant will be given several days to pack his bags and move out. If the tenant fails to move, then and only then can the landlord hire a marshal to physically remove the tenant and his possessions from the premises. Typically, the landlord then changes the lock and rents to a new and hopefully more financially responsible tenant.

Another more English term for eviction is that used in Downton Abbey, "foreclose on the lease."

APPLICATION TO DA: Given that the Drewes were significantly late in their rent, Robert had good grounds to evict them. Had Robert sought a court order to remove the Drewes from occupancy, he would have been successful.

However, a lease is a contract, an agreement between two parties, and as such can typically be modified if both parties are willing. In this circumstance, and with some coaxing by the younger Drewe, both parties were willing to adjust the due date of the rent and forego eviction. Most landlords are less forgiving, and understandably so. Leases are business transactions in which landlords expect to receive rent on a regular basis, enabling them to cover their expenses associated with the property,

Chapter 60

Free Speech: Fighting Words – Branson

A FACTS:[8] Branson sided with rebels in uprisings against the English aristocracy in colonial Ireland. He was reportedly present at various republican meetings when violence was advocated. As a result, he was a wanted man and fled to Downton Abbey to avoid prosecution. Robert was able to arrange for Branson to avoid consequences on the condition that Branson did not return to Ireland.

US LAW: Criminal statutes often outlaw threats of harm. Nonetheless, the constitutional right of free speech protects most expression and criticism, even if hateful and even if couched in offensive terminology. In a famous case during the Vietnam War period, *Cohen v. California*, the United States Supreme Court, the highest court in the country, determined that the expression "Fuck the draft" was protected speech.

Threatening comments however cross the line from protected to unprotected when they constitutes *fighting words*, meaning expression likely to incite immediate violence. Confusion exists in the law concerning what exactly constitutes fighting words. Case law is inconsistent. Law is sometimes inexact, and

---

[8] This situation is also examined from a different legal perspective in Chapter 47.

this is one of those areas. But the following guideline can be gleaned. The more threatening the words are, and the more imminent is the threatened violence, the greater the likelihood the communication will be considered unprotected fighting words.

APPLICATION TO DA: To determine if Branson and others present at the meetings could be liable for advocating violence against the government would depend on whether their comments constituted fighting words. If the protestors were discussing various methods of resistance, one of which was violence, and they were developing plans on how to proceed, that would not constitute fighting words. If however they were readying the group to proceed immediately to engage in violent acts, the speech would be unprotected.

Chapter 61

Medical Malpractice: Failure to Diagnose – Dr. Tapsell

A FACTS: Sadly, Lady Sybil Branson (nee Crawley) died in childbirth. The cause of her death was eclampsia, a rare but serious condition that causes seizures during pregnancy and in rare cases, is fatal.

As Sybil went into labor, Dr. Clarkson, the family doctor, noted that she was experiencing symptoms of preeclampsia – swollen ankles, dizziness, shortness of breath, and excess protein in her urine. Clarkson advocated for Sybil to have a C-section as soon as possible to save her life. If delivery by a mother exhibiting signs of preeclampsia is delayed, the risk of eclampsia increases. Dr. Tapsell, a specialist, insisted that the symptoms were normal signs of childbirth and so failed to treat the condition. Robert Crawley sided with Dr. Tapsell and rejected a C-section. Unfortunately, Dr. Clarkson was correct. Failure to follow his recommendation proved fatal.

US LAW: A doctor who is negligent (careless) in the practice of medicine will be liable to patients injured thereby, based on medical malpractice. Examples include improper treatment (for example, failure to prescribe needed medication), failure to warn of known risks of a procedure or course of treatment (for example, failure to inform a patient that a recommended procedure could cause undesirable side effects), and failure to detect and diagnose a medical problem. In the latter category, if a competent doctor would have discovered the patient's illness or made a different diagnosis which would have led to a better outcome, the doctor who misdiagnosed or failed to detect will be liable for medical malpractice.

When determining liability, doctors are expected to match that level of care, skill and treatment that is recognized as acceptable and appropriate among similarly situated physicians.

In many states, before a patient can sue for malpractice, she must participate in a hearing before a medical malpractice review panel. The panel hears arguments, reviews evidence and expert testimony, and then determines whether malpractice has occurred. The tribunal's decision is not binding. The panel's purpose is to help weed out unfounded medical malpractice claims by discouraging plaintiffs with weak cases from proceeding in court. However, if the case goes to trial, the panel's decision can be introduced as evidence by the party it favors.

APPLICATION TO DA: Dr. Tapsell overlooked the symptoms of preeclampsia and as a result Sybil lost her life. This is the stuff of which medical malpractice cases are made. If Sybil's family sues, they will have to prove that failure by Tapsell to detect the preeclampsia symptoms falls below the level of care, skill and treatment recognized as acceptable and appropriate among obstetricians practicing in the same or similar location and time as Dr. Tapsell and Downton Abbey.

Chapter 62

Voting Rights for Women – Edith

DA FACTS: Not long after Edith's wedding was cancelled at the last minute, she became involved in the women's rights movement. Women could not yet vote in England. She expressed her concerns about this circumstance in a letter-to-the-editor of a newspaper. The communication was not only published, but it was so well received Edith became a weekly columnist. Her advocacy and that of others like her were partially successful in 1918 with the passage of the English Representation of the People Act which gave landed women over 30 the right to vote.

US LAW: Women were disenfranchised in the United States until the adoption of the 19th Amendment to the Constitution in 1920. The new rule prohibited the government from denying any Unites States citizen the right to vote on the basis of gender. The Amendment guaranteed that all women would have the right to cast their ballot. The change in the law was the long time goal of the suffrage movement, led by Susan B. Anthony. Advocacy endured for decades and took many forms including lectures, writings, marches, lobbying, petitioning, picketing, parading and civil disobedience. Supporters often faced strong opposition by aggressive hecklers who occasionally became violent. The work of the indefatigable suffragettes paid off when the Amendment was ratified.

Eight years later England followed suit. The Representation of the People Act, also called the Equal Franchise Act, gave all women over age 21 the right to vote.

APPLICATION TO DA: If Lady Edith was a citizen of the United States today she, like all other male and female citizens, could cast a ballot in every election.

Appendices

Appendix A

Introduction to Law

DEFINITION. What is this thing called law? Perhaps the most understandable definition is this: a body of rules with which people must comply or face penalties. Additional meanings include a set of rules used by judges to decide disputes, and a method to control people's conduct. Common to all of these definitions is the idea that law affects our live everyday in significant ways. Law requires that we conform our behavior to certain expected norms and if we do not, we face unpleasant consequences.

SOURCES OF LAW. From where does our law come? There are four sources:

1. The Federal Constitution
2. Statutes adopted by legislators
3. Common law, created by judges
4. Government agency regulations

CONSTITUTIONAL LAW. The law embodied in the United States Constitution is called Constitutional Law. It prescribes the organization of the federal government – including the executive, legislative and judicial branches – and defines the powers of the government. The Constitution establishes vital legal rights, called the Bill of Rights. These include freedom of speech, freedom of religion, right to a fair trial, right to an attorney, right against cruel and unusual punishment, and more.

STATUTES. These are laws promulgated by *legislators*, who are elected lawmakers. We all vote for legislators at the federal, state, and local levels. Each level of government has different topics on which law makers *legislate* (make laws). For example, the Federal Government legislates on such issues as national security, federal crimes (criminal activity involving more than one state, such as transporting a kidnapping victim across state lines), and business transactions that impact more than one state. State legislators pass laws addressing matters such as speed limits on state roads, state crimes (criminal activity occurring wholly within one state), and child neglect and abuse. City and town legislators adopt laws dealing with such topics as leash laws (requiring dogs to be on a leash when away from their owners' property), and restrictions on the permissible noise level at a home or business.

COMMON LAW. This refers to legal rules that originate from decisions written by judges that address issues raised in lawsuits. Judges' decisions clarify the law when the Constitution or the wording of a statute is ambiguous.

GOVERNMENT AGENCY REGULATIONS. *Government agencies* are units of government with administrative responsibilities. Each agency oversees a particular industry and may have authority to make law binding on that industry. Agencies are created because our society is very complex and legislators do not have the required expertise to adopt laws on all facets of life. Examples of government agencies include the Consumer Product Safety Commission which enforces regulations designed to ensure the safety of consumer products, and the Environmental Protection Agency which is charged with safeguarding our environment. The term *regulations* refers to law created by a government agency.

Appendix B

Wills and Estates

WILLS. A *will* is a document in which people state how they want their property to be distributed upon their death. A person who creates a will is called a *testator*. In most states a will, to be valid, must be signed by the testator in the presence of two witnesses. They then sign a document swearing to the fact that the testator not only signed the will, but reviewed it in their presence and stated that the will accurately reflects the testator's wishes. Additionally, the witnesses will attest that the testator is of sound mind.

In the will, the testator can make gifts of specific property to a variety of people. Gifts of personal property are called *bequests*. A gift of *real property* (land and buildings) is called a *devise*. A testator can also make donations in a will to various charitable organizations.

The testator is well-advised to include contingent beneficiaries, people who will inherit if the primary beneficiary predeceases the testator.

TRUST. A will might include a *trust*, meaning an arrangement in which a third person, called a trustee, holds and manages money and/or other assets for the benefit of a beneficiary. The trustee has a fiduciary duty to the beneficiary, meaning a legal duty to act solely for the beneficiary's interest. A trust would typically be used when a beneficiary is too young to manage money or is a known spendthrift.

PROBATE. When the testator dies, the will is submitted to probate, meaning the process of proving the validity of the will in court and overseeing the distribution to the heirs of the deceased's property, consistent with the directives in the will.

INTESTATE. If a person dies without a will, he is said to die intestate. In such circumstance, state law specifies how the property will be allocated. Generally, the closest relative takes all, but if the deceased person is survived by multiples of the same level relative (for example, no spouse, three children), they will split equally the property in the estate..

Appendix C

Differences Between Civil and Criminal Law

All law can be classified as either criminal or civil. The four main differences between the two, explained in detail below, are:

1. The remedy sought
2. The name of the plaintiff
3. The attorney for the plaintiff
4. The burden of proof.

REMEDY. In a criminal case, the remedy sought by the plaintiff is punishment of the wrongdoer, and often rehabilitation. In a civil case, the remedy is compensation (money) for an injury.

NAME OF PLAINTIFF. There are usually two parties to a lawsuit, although there may be more. The two are called the plaintiff and the defendant. The plaintiff is the one who has a complaint against the defendant and initiates the lawsuit. The defendant is the party who the plaintiff sues, seeking a remedy for an alleged violation of law. In a criminal case, the plaintiff is society-at-large, not just the complainant (the person injured). The plaintiff's name in every criminal case is "The People of the State of _____", or "The People of the Commonwealth of _____". In a civil case, the name of the plaintiff is the person who was harmed.

PLAINTIFF'S ATTORNEY. In a criminal case, society is represented by a prosecutor, often called a district attorney. Prosecutors' salaries are paid by the government. In a civil case, plaintiffs hire and pay for their own lawyer.

BURDEN OF PROOF. In both civil and criminal cases, for plaintiffs to win, they must convince the jury of the truth of their claim to a specified degree of certainty. In a criminal case, the degree required is beyond a reasonable doubt. This is a very high standard. If a juror has a reasonable doubt about defendant's guilt or liability, the juror must vote for not guilty. In a civil case, the burden of proof is significantly less. It is a preponderance of the evidence, which means only that the jury must be more than 50 percent sure. The reason for the difference is that in a criminal case, a person's freedom is at stake, while in a civil case, only money is at risk. As a society, we value freedom significantly more than money.

Appendix D

Criminal Law Issues

Understanding some aspects of criminal law will facilitate your understanding of this book. Discussed in this Appendix are the following:

1. The difference between felonies and misdemeanors
2. Degreeing factors
3. Defenses
4. Sentencing

FELONY AND MISDEMEANOR. Crimes are divided into two categories for purposes of distinguishing serious conduct from less serious conduct. A felony is the more serious crime. The time in jail faced by a perpetrator who commits a felony is, in most states, more than one year and could be life. Examples of felonies include assault resulting in serious injury, grand larceny (stealing a large amount of money; in some states, more than $1,000), and robbery (stealing personal property from a person by the use of force or a weapon).

A misdemeanor is a lower level crime for which the maximum time in jail in most states is one year. Examples of misdemeanors include stealing limited amounts of money, hitting a person causing injury but not serious injury, and the first time someone is convicted of driving while intoxicated (in some states, a second conviction is a felony).

A third category of wrongful conduct exists in criminal law called a violation. It involves illegal behavior less serious than a misdemeanor. Usually the maximum jail time is 15 days. An example is harassment, which includes pushing or shoving someone without causing injury.

DEGREEING FACTORS. Most crimes have degreeing factors. These are circumstances that make the crime more serious. Examples of degreeing factors include the seriousness of an injury for assault, the amount of money stolen for larceny, the use of a weapon while committing certain crimes such as robbery, and prior conviction(s) of the same crime.

DEFENSES. A defense is an explanation for illegal conduct that, if proven, relieves the actor of liability. An example is self-defense. Customarily, if you use force against another person and cause injury, you are liable for the crime of assault. However, if the reason you used the force was to defend yourself from an attack by the person you injured, a defense of self-defense may apply, which would result in the assault charge against you being dismissed.

SENTENCING. A sentence is the punishment imposed on a defendant convicted of a crime. A sentence will consist of one or more of the following components: imprisonment; death (in some states only); a fine; home confinement; community service (defendant must perform volunteer work to benefit a charitable agency in the community); various kinds of treatment including drugs, alcohol, anger management, domestic violence, and values clarification; conditional discharge (the defendant must comply with specified conditions such as not repeating the criminal activity); probation (defendant is supervised by a probation officer with whom defendant must meet periodically and report progress in school, employment, and treatment); and more. Sentences are determined by the judge except in death penalty cases when the jury decides whether to impose the death penalty or life without parole.

Appendix E

Court Jurisdiction

The term jurisdiction refers to the authority of a court to hear cases. Most courts have limited authority, meaning they hear only certain types of lawsuits. For example, Surrogate Court, also called Probate Court, has jurisdiction to hear only cases involving wills and estates. Family Court has authority to hear only cases involving family issues such as adoption or child neglect. Neither court has jurisdiction to hear, for example, a case about a plaintiff who tripped and fell in a restaurant and is suing for compensation for a broken arm.

Numerous classifications of jurisdiction exist. For example, a court has either original or appellate jurisdiction, and a few courts have both. A court with original jurisdiction hears cases the first time they are heard by a court. Trials are held in courts with original jurisdiction. Appellate jurisdiction refers to the authority of a court to hear appeals. An appeal is the process of an appellate court reviewing a decision of the court that previously heard the case. An appellate court may affirm the prior court's decision (uphold it), reverse the decision, or return the case to the original court for further proceedings.

www.ingramcontent.com/pod-product-compliance
Lightning Source LLC
Chambersburg PA
CBHW070242190526
45169CB00001B/267